Voices of Today

3

Anthologies of modern verse
edited by F.E.S. Finn

The Albemarle Books of Modern Verse I and II
Poets of our Time
Poems of the Sixties
Here and Human

Voices of Today

An anthology of recent verse

selected by F.E.S. Finn

John Murray

Printed in Great Britain by Martins of Berwick

0 7195 3757 6

Contents

SOCIETY

RELIGION

WAR

SPACE

NARRATIVE

Preface

All poetry reflects the society in which it is written; sometimes this happens incidentally, but more often poets set out to portray the spirit of their age. This can be seen in their attitudes not only to the present but also to the future and to the past. A short anthology cannot hope to include poems about all aspects of today's scene any more than it can include contributions from all contemporary poets. But an attempt has been made to include poems dealing with important topics of the day, poems written in a variety of styles ranging from the lyrical to the narrative.

A prominent figure in the educational world, speaking not too seriously perhaps, described contemporary Britain as 'a pools win, sin bin, wimpy bar, two car, first name, loose dame, rolling stone, ansaphone, loud sound, sleep around, disco scenes, tight jeans, colour telly, slingawelly, page threes, deep freeze, opt out, be a lout, dull void, unemployed type of society'. This dissatisfaction with our way of life appears in much of today's verse. The confidence and hope of Shelley's 'If Winter comes, can Spring be far behind?' rarely finds a voice. The 'nature' poetry of recent years is still concerned with the beauty as well as the violence and cruelty of nature; but increasingly poets show an awareness of how the beauty of our countryside and our towns is under threat from 'progress' and development. The meaning of the word 'pollution', in fact, has been enlarged in the last decade to cover almost any kind of damage to the environment; and it is in this broader sense that it appears as one of the topic headings of this book.

The section headings in this book must not be thought of as hard and fast divisions, for many poems which appear in one section might well be transferred to another. What I have tried to avoid, however, is the allocation of a poem to a section simply on account of its title.

Although this book is arranged according to topics, there is an alphabetical list of poets with the numbers of the pages on which their poems appear. This enables the reader to study poets in addition to topics. Many of the poems have not been published before; all the others have been written or collected in book form since 1970.

The Poet's Tongue

With industry and patience he must bring
Together his great arsenal which stores
Blunt cudgels with the very latest thing,
Romantic swords employed in ancient wars
And complicated engines needing great
Skill and practice to manipulate.

And he must travel far in time and space,
Find loot in labs and factories, soil and sand,
Arrange his plunder in well-ordered ways
So what he needs will always be at hand.
And yet, possessing such elaborate means,
He'll constantly invite a puzzled stare
By using—not his intricate machines—
But bits of flint that hit the target square.

Vernon Scannell

Memories of Childhood

Comprehending It Not

December, 1921. Seven years of age,
And my mother dead—the house in mourning,
The shop shut up for Christmas—I
Was fobbed off to my Grandma's with my Christmas Tree
Bundled under my arm. Out
In the brown packed streets the lamplight drizzled down
On squirming pavements; the after-smell of war
Clung like a fungus to wall and windowsill,
And the backyards reeked of poverty. Boys,
Their big toes squirting through their boots,
Growled out *While Shepherds Watched* to deaf door-knobs,
And the Salvation Army—euphoniums slung, un-playing—
Stumped the length of the town at the thump of a drum
To cracked Hallelujahs in the Market Square.

I edged past muttering entries, sidled inside the lobby,
And slammed the door on the dark. My Grandma
Banged the door with her stick to greet me,
Tossed me a humbug and turned again to the goose,
Spluttering on the kitchen range. My four rough uncles
Barged jokily around in flannel shirtsleeves,
Challenged to comic fisticuffs or gripped me
With a wrestler's grip and hyped me and cross-buttocked
In Cumberland-and-Westmorland style—till puffed,
    at last, and weary
Of horse-play and of me, they ripped my Christmas
Tree from its wrapper, unfolded its gaunt
Umbrella frame of branches, stuck candles in the green raffia,
And stood it on the dresser, well out of my reach.

1

I crouched down by the fire, crunching my humbug,
And scissoring holly and bells from coloured card;
The huff of the smoke brought water to my eyes,
The smell of the goose made me retch. Then suddenly,
The gas plopped out and the house was doused in darkness—
A break in the main and not a chance of repair
Till the day after Boxing Day. Matches rattled;
A twist of paper torn from *The Daily Mail*
Relayed the flame from grate to candle,
And soon, high on the dresser, my Christmas Tree,
Ignited like a gorse-bush, pollened the room with light.

Proud as a proselyte,
I stuffed white wax in the mouth of a medicine bottle,
Pioneered the wild lobby and the attic stairs
And dared the heathen flagstones of the yard,
Bearing my gleam of a gospel. At the scratch of a match,
Christmas crackled up between winter walls,
And Grandma's house was home, her sharp voice called in
    kindness,
And the fists no longer frightened. Tickled at the trick of it,
I 'Merry-Christmas-ed' gas-pipe, gas and gas men,
'God-blessed' the darkness and pulled crackers with the cold—
Scarcely aware what it was that I rejoiced in:
Whether the black-out or the candles,
Whether the light or the dark.

Norman Nicholson

St John's School

When I went back the school was rather small
but not unexpectedly or oddly so.
I peered in at the windows of the hall
where we sang O God Our Help thirty years ago
for D-Day, the Normandy landings. It was all
as I'd pictured it. Outside, they'd cut the row

of dusty laurels, laid a lawn instead,
and the prefab classroom at the end was new;
but there were the lavatories, there was the shed
where we sat on rainy days with nothing to do,
giggling; and the beech-trees overhead
whose fallen husks we used to riffle through

for triangular nuts. Yes, all as it should be—
no false images to negotiate,
no shocks. I wandered off contentedly
across the playground, out through the north gate,
down the still knee-straining slope, to see
what sprang up suddenly across the street:

the church, that had hardly existed in my past,
that had lurked behind a tree or two, unknown—
and uncensorious of me as I chased
squirrels over the graves—the church had grown:
high on its huge mound it soared, vast;
and God glared out from behind a tombstone.

Fleur Adcock

Middle Infant

I sat on the long form
and sponged my slate
while the terrible Miss McCleery
wagged her cane in front.
The smell of jerseys, crumbs, ink,
the sound of screeching chalk
and the firmly shut windows
established her kingdom.

A Middle Infant now
released from the chanting tiers,
I was edging my way
out into life.
The years would give me
height, words, problems;
She, in her black tight carapace,
would stay there for ever.

John Hewitt

For What We Have Received

We were not vegetarian from choice
but from necessity; meat cost too much
and allotment salad seemed free.

So there were fragile young
lettuces in season and small
shining globes of radishes,
spring onions which chilled
the throat (jibbons we called them)
and deep purple flesh of beetroot
fleetingly reminding us of meat.

In autumn we finished our meal
with blackberry pudding or wimberry pie
whichever fruit our eager indigo fingers
had picked that golden day.
My mother had a hand for pastry,
which my sisters vainly emulated,
especially for apple tart
made on a large flat dish
and served geometrically neat
and dry, not spoilt with custard.

In winter we had a thinner time:
sometimes dinner was half a banana
with bread and margarine, though
there was always tea, hot, strong and sweet.
All week we waited for the Sunday joint.
The smell of mint or parsley
can still arouse in me
the excitement we felt
for the small sweet mountain mutton
when it arrived on our table.

Shoulder of lamb with its crisp
brown crust of fat across the top
or breast of lamb, fragrant
with green parsley stuffing
speckled with herbs and chopped
onion, was served with spring greens
and yellow waxy new potatoes
tiny from our own garden.
But the meat was the thing;
we were not vegetarian from choice.

Tom Earley

The Harbour

Our school was by a harbour;
in the lunch-hour one hot day
a group of us went for a stroll along the shore.
We walked below the narrow wall
on ochre-coloured shingle set in clay,
along the hard shore grass
in tussocks webbed with weed
and the shells of mollusc and crustacean;
flotsam laced the tide-line, silver-grey
like dry-point sketches of the bones of things.
Below the pebbles there were larger stones,
between the tides, in mud just firm enough
to stand on, slithery; and further out
towards the banks of reed where wildfowl
   nested,
there were the mudflaps where a skin of
   grey-green slime
filmed unfathomable depths
of oilblack mud.
              Inevitably
we began to search
beneath the larger stones for 'things',
for eels or shrimps or blenny—anything
that moved or tried to hide—but most of all
we sought the green shore crabs,
collecting them in washed-up tins and in our
   caps,
delighted that, confined, they clawed each
   other.
              All our shoes
were mired with mud, our hands with weed.
The sun shone warmly on our backs.
The waiting gulls wheeled round above us
as we played, predicting that
where boys and nature meet there will be
   pickings.
'Let's race them,' somebody suggested,
so we lined the wrigglers up below the wall,
perhaps four dozen on the starting line.
Some hurried for the distant sea;
most started digging in. We tried
to spur them on with little shoves,

but they were not competitors from choice.
In his frustration, one of us,
dropping a stone to get his charger going,
mis-aimed and trapped its leg.
The crab pulled free without the leg
and ran. The rest of us, therefore,
urged ours with stones, deliberately
maiming them. The crabs took flight—
in minutes they would disappear
into the mud and stones,
and our diversion with them.
                    Instantly,
'Let's bomb them', we decided.
Hurriedly collecting bigger stones,
we climbed the harbour wall and as the crabs
scuttled and scrabbled down the beach,
we sent our missiles crashing down on them.
Like armoured cars and tanks,
they scattered blindly, zig-zag, blundering,
hurling themselves against the vanished sea.
                    Triumphantly,
we spread that sector of the bay
with twitching legs and claws—dismembered
    shells
broke up like addled eggs across the stones.
None reached the water, all were smashed
or left just not alive enough to entertain.

Today that wasted edge of land
has largely been reclaimed;
the battlefield is under concrete now
being profitably used to hold a motorway—
except for that impossible expanse of mud
reluctantly reserved
for migrant waterfowl. There is no shore,
and my successors have no crabs
to slaughter in an idle hour
before they go to Maths.

Cal Clothier

September Journey

At last I have arrived.
The streets, as close as vines,
Blue-grey in fading light,
Walls in the history
Of gospel and coal mine.

I stop the car,
Relax, and breathe the air
That holds the mining dust
That blacked my face.
But that was thirty years ago.

Town Clock still serves
As a memorial to heroes
Of two wars, its bronze apron
An inventory of Welsh names.
It strikes the hours in melancholy tones.

I drag myself out of my car
By Maggie's shop.
The Cherry Blossom ads.,
Too high for vandals,
Are still visible.

The shop is locked and empty.
I often as a boy stood by
The oak counter and watched
As Maggie worked her butter pats
Among the bottles now collectors' items.

On the shop's skull the trading name
Has faded to a delicate tone.
In the abandoned rooms
The silence is confessional
With a blessing of memories.

I walk along as private as a stranger
And wince at derelict chapels.
No singers in the streets
Only chains of cars,
The images of prosperity.

I feel the nervous air
Of a dramatic place.
Each window, wall and door
Are historyprints of special times.
Everywhere a ghost in altar shadows

With names written
In sacrificial dust.
Blessed are the bygone miners,
Their Spartan histories
Have faded like the dead chapels.

Abandoned friends of gangdays
Are lean and jaded in their fifties.
Remember all the mining graft
Through innocent days
Of marvellous youth?

This place, ugly and beautiful,
Dust-freckled and worn,
Terraced-packed with fools and talents,
Buries its scars and heroes
In poems of daily life and certainty.

Robert Morgan

Hornets and Adders

I

When I was a boy I lived at Brockenhurst
In the New Forest,
One of the few places
Where there are still hornets.

Ten, I was told could kill a horse
And five a man.
Then, there were adders, too,
And an old adder-hunter,

Brusher Mills, who lived wild,
Was impervious to their bites,
And caught them for hospitals
The venom being useful for heart-patients.

8

II

And once above a little stream
Where you could catch the sluggish
Stone-loach; or trout-fry; or millers-thumbs;
(The water clear over gravel)

I watched a fight to the death
Between two hornets, fearsome
Gold and purple insects twice
As big as a queen wasp.

They grappled and fell dead
Into the stream. I fished them out
A little timorously, though I knew
Their venom was in each other.

III

That clash has never left my vision.
I hear it, see it, know its inexorable
And futile end. In 1940
Above the same stream, but higher,

A Spitfire grappled with a Dornier.
I heard the grunting of their shot-up engines,
Saw the pillar of smoke by Stoney Cross,
Knew them all dead, their venom in each other.

IV

Often I think of these sights and sounds
And that old man who couldn't
Read or write, who smelt, and lived on berries
Roots and a bit of poaching.

But he was skilled enough to extract
Snake-venom, bottle it and sell it,
(Though not for much) to help save
People far off in high white beds

He would never know. I find
I am grievous for something lost
Men seem to be glad to have lost
I can't think why.

9

It is really very easy
To catch a stone-loach—tricky
With a trout—then, all you do
Is look at them, lithe in your fingers,

And put them back in. As I write this
I think of other people's
Feelings and thoughts and the sound of Birmingham
And the fox that watched my fishing.

V

I was young then. I knew nothing
Of the perverse stupidities of men
And insects, and still I am aghast
At hornets, politicians.

Mysteries of fact so seeming clear,
Yet held in the hand one instant
Above the stream too unreal
To be so vicious, meaning it or no.

Patric Dickinson

Recollections of a Feudal Childhood

Our gardener swilled his elevenses
From a cracked cup kept for the purpose
In the kitchen cupboard. This was not
On account of his having anything contagious
My mother explained, it was simply because
He expected a cracked cup—

But I was eight. I went and asked him
Why he expected it—why was it kept
In the kitchen? Did he know about
The ones we gave our visitors, a complete set
Kept in the dining room, with saucers
And plates of the same pattern?

10

And did he know (for the fit was on me)
That our teaspoons were real silver,
That our fish-knives had pearl handles
And our napkins rings of polished leather,
Did he? But I came back to the point, again
I asked about the cracked cup.

He smiled. I think he might have answered
But my mother called me in
To wash my hands and lay the table,
That was my job, she explained, the garden
His. Then, after lunch, I helped clear up;
Back on its shelf went the cracked cup.

John Mole

Old Movies

How I loved those old movies
they would show in the Roxys
and Regals amongst all that
gilt plaster, or in the Bijou
flea-pits smelling of Jeyes.
The men sleek haired and suited,
with white cuffs and big trilbies,
their girls all pushovers,
wide-eyed with lashes
like venus fly traps and their
clouds of blonde candyfloss
for hair. Oh those bosoms, hips
and those long long legs
I never saw in daylight!
And their apartments,
vast as temples,
full of unused furniture,
the sideboards bending with booze,
and all those acres of bed!
She, in attendance, wearing
diaphanous, but never quite
diaphanous enough, nightwear.

11

And their lives!
Where the baddies only,
if not always, stopped one,
and they loved and loved
and never ended up married.
Every time I get a whiff
of that disinfectant
I feel nostalgic.

John Cotton

Humour

I, Sardine

First a great shadow appeared,
Then a bright light
Haloed the roof of our world,
Drawing us up
Till we were caught in the net.

In the world of the Gods
We could not breathe
The ethereal air,
But through Their great mercy
Our gaspings were soon ended.

Lovingly were we anointed
And laid in holy oils;
Ten of us, in a silver casket,
There to be sealed in
Until One with a golden key
Should open the box
And we be made whole
To dwell in the world above
For ever and ever.

Frank Wood

The Goldfish Speaks from Beyond the Grave

Twelve years swimming from
one side of that tank to the other,
bumping my nose against the glass,
turning around, flicking a fin,
and bumping it again. Christ, if they
only knew how boring it all was.
The same food dropped in each day,
the water changed once a week.
They couldn't even let me live in
darkness, so insistent were they
about knowing what I was doing.
And when I was dying, and wanted to
lie at the bottom of the tank, they
rapped on the glass, and pushed
their squirming faces against it.
The horror is that there is no horror,
but there is certainly despair,
and I knew what that was all about.
Well, it's finished at last,
and I've been buried in the garden.
A perfect end for an English fish,
helping to push up the weeds, so that
the family will have something else
to worry about each Sunday morning.

Jim Burns

The Text

'If you are good,' said my aunt,
'You can put your hand in my little box of secrets,
And draw out a present for yourself.'

I was very good, as people generally are
When there's a reward in the offing.
I didn't kick the cat, though I still didn't like it;
I didn't bang the doors;
Everywhere I went, I went on tiptoe:
I even remembered manners at the table,
And didn't drink until I'd finished eating.

Then, after tea, my aunt brought out her box,
And said, 'Now close your eyes! Take a lucky dip!'
There was nothing but paper in it, but I hoped
It might be a note, ten shillings or even a pound.
But what do you think I got? A mouldy text!
Nothing but words on a piece of yellow paper,
'Remember the Lord in the days of thy transgression.'
Not even sixpence, just a bit from the Bible.

I pretended to be grateful. But I was mad.
The only word I saw was the word 'transgression'.
I clattered over the kitchen, and banged the door,
I tore up the paper and threw it in the rhubarb,
And gave the cat a kick it will never forget.

And the last person I thought of was the Lord.

F. Grice

The Bible

Everyone in prison reads the Bible.
If they never wanted to before
They do now: it is an unwritten law.

To prisoners of war the journalist
Offered to send it and a home-made cake.
With loved ones far away you pray and bake.

The swindler starting on his five-year sentence
Reads a portion as he always has
Done, every single day, so his wife says.

A TV documentary about
A certain prison showed the earnest chaplain
Getting the first offender to explain

What he would like. 'A Bi—' 'Yes?' He could not
Believe his ears. 'A Biro' stammered the con.
'Oh yes, of course. Of course I'll get you one.'

Patricia Beer

Tom Cat

Tom cat, you have
a heathen heart.
You love to tear
live things apart.

To save you from
this mortal sin
I feed you dead ones
from a tin,

and round your neck
I hang a bell.
But still you have
a heathen smell.

So I shall take you
to the vet.
We'll make a christian
of you, yet.

Sydney Carter

Roundabout

The woman turned and looked back.
    She became a pillar of salt.
The man turned and looked back.
    He lost his wife.
The boy turned and looked back.
    He lost his future.
The girl turned and looked back.
    She lost her honour.
The climber turned and looked back.
    He lost his foothold.
The M.P. turned and looked back.
    He lost his seat.
The priest turned and looked back.
    He lost his faith.

The King turned and looked back.
He lost his head.
The Prime Minister turned and looked back.
He sold his memoirs for millions.

Ronald Bottrall

If You Ask a Welshman to Dinner

If you ask a Welshman to dinner,
hide all the silver first,
remove the tube from the television set,
lock up your bottles
and your husband's clean shirts.
Any faggots, black pudding, kippers,
        laver bread, cold sausages, Caerphilly
        cheese or tomato ketchup
that may be lying about
seal in the fridge.
Put barbed wire round your history books.
Before he sits down, ask him to take
the leeks out of his ears, to remove
the two nuts of coal dangling from his nostrils, and to drop
the rugby pill he is clutching.
On no account request him to pronounce
that place with the bloody long name in North Wales.
Then relieve him of the flagon in his right pocket,
the hymn-book and emaciated volume of passionate verse
in his left, the gelignite sticks for bridge-blowing in his topcoat
(but do not touch his Collected Thoughts of Saunders Lewis).
Explain the conventional use of the knife and fork,
ask him if he knows Barry Island.
If you stuff a dishcloth in his mouth
he should be unable to sing 'Land of My Fathers'.
And if you've remembered to mine the front lawn,
hired a bouncer from Soho,
and posted your neighbour with a machine-gun at the back—
you might just be able to enjoy
a very pleasant, memorable evening . . .

John Tripp

Camel

Deferentially, through the door, my butler approaches
Silently stepping across the mohair rug in plastic shoes
And waiting silently for me to put down the book I wasn't reading.
Sir, he says quietly, as I raise my head and one eyebrow,
There is, sir, a person at the door wishing to sell you a lame camel.

Nothing any more surprises me. Men have walked on the moon,
And poured defoliant upon innocent trees.
Flying saucers have been sighted and an eminent film star has
                              refused the offer of an Oscar.
Nothing, therefore, but nothing can surprise me by surprising me.

At my door there stands a person wishing to sell me a lame camel.
And why should there not be. Am I not worthy to be regarded
As the proper recipient, in exchange for old pounds and
                              new pence, no doubt,
Of a lame camel. I can certainly afford to run one.
Who says I may, can, should not run one on my income?

Sitting there I whip myself into a frenzy of hatred for those,
For anyone who should dare to think I cannot afford a lame camel.
Who are they, I shout to myself, who are they to set up
                              such economic criteria
That shall preclude me from the ownership of a lame camel?

I am bursting with anger, effervescing to myself with loathing.
I stand up, lay the book down flatly on my escritoire.
I half-turn from that elegant piece of furniture.
I address myself with the utmost coolness, incredibly controlled,
                              to my butler.

Tell him, I say in tones of complete certainty,
Tell him I already have one.

D. W. Broadbridge

People

Microscopics
(Tangier, Morocco)

The dove on a string, a gift
from his father,
flapped and was dragged
across the hotel floor,
a child's living toy.

The frightened huff froze white
in the waiting room of our gaze,
we made for it a future
of our questions.
Then up started the girl,
rifling indignations
through her silks.
She knew just what to do, always,
had a way of adjusting
for any passing cause
the wandering beauty
of her face.
'More wine!' She doused
her bread, dispensed solutions,
and cursed the pleading boy.
'I snatch the bird,
fling wide the shutters
and tip it at the sky!'

Seven storeys below freedom
a plaything panicked among
its own blood and feathers.

'My bird have wings no fly,
father break him the wings,'
he said in our language.
'Wings are clipped.'

Nigel Jenkins

An Attitude of Mind

Heat bounced off the cobbled yard
And hit us in the eyes, already bleared
By the sun to a constant blink.
Starlings showered down onto the barn,
Dipped through the door, paused, and sprayed up again,
Ceaselessly. Dust twirled slowly; a tractor stank.

Tod took a tennis racket, and flicked
It from hand to hand. You've picked
A good time, he said. I'll demonstrate.
The barn was heavy with hay smell
And all in it invisible
When Tod swung the doors together, tight.

In the dimness hovered small echoings,
The whirring motors of starlings' wings,
Soft and confusing, and right up,
Where the nests were, raucous twitters.
We stood till things assembled round us,
Colouring themselves and taking shape:

A spiked machine, blue plastic sacks
Of nitro-chalk, a couple of hayforks,
A three-wheeled pram. Heavy beams
Hung over us, streaked white like the walls
Up at the top amid squalls
Of bird noise. Tod flung wide his arms

And shook his muscles loose, and took
A good grip on his racket. With a kick
He broke some pebbles free, and flung one
Up at the roof, then another, then more,
And they clunked about on the wood up there
Before the sharp drop back onto stone.

And down came the starlings, beating about
In a bewildered way, at head height and waist height,
Dozens of them, whizzing so close they missed
Us by the width of their wind. Tod was using
The racket, swinging from the shoulder, not pausing
At all, grunting and moving very fast.

Blow after blow vibrated those strings.
Bodies rocketed to stillness, and there were shufflings
And dragging movements everywhere,
As birds, beaks broken, necks half-unscrewed,
Flapped untidily and slowly clawed
A small circular progress on the floor.

Tod stamped on these but others escaped to the roof
In the end and sat safe. Tod gave a laugh
At his last futile swipes and looked
Round at the litter of feathers, at the wrecks
Of birds and bits of birds, at the marks
On the walls where birds had split and cracked.

The nearest bodies he nudged with the toe of his boot
To a neat heap, and he scooped with his racket
Several more to throw in; he was deft, accurate.
Hungry nests wheezed still. They'll soon starve,
That lot, Tod said, stroking his ear with the curve
Of his racket. Tomorrow in here will be dead quiet.

He opened the doors and the daylight fell
In, hot and dazzling. A good haul,
He said, licking sweat, wiping an eye, puzzled
At my silence. Pests they are from the minute they hatch.
It's all an attitude of mind. He raised an arm to scratch.
Down the words Dunlop Junior dark blood drizzled.

John Cassidy

Song of the Hand

The fulmar justifies its flight.
From lusty action heroes spring.
Wherever works of art are wrought
in oils or stone or crystal thought,
the curves of beauty and delight
were featured first in arm and wing.

21

Though men may gather from the earth
where others toiled in wind and rain,
and nations honour sleight of mind
more than the craftsman's skill of hand,
the power that tames a mountain's girth
flows from the hand and not the brain.

Howard Sergeant

Navvy

The moleskins stiff as bark,
the drill grafting his wrists
to the shale:
where the surface is weavy

and the camber tilts
in the slow lane, he stands
waving you down. The morass
the macadam snakes over

swallowed his yellow bulldozer
four years ago, laying it down
with lake-dwellings and dug-outs,
pike-shafts, axe-heads, bone pins,

all he is indifferent to.
He has not relented
under weather or insults,
my brother and keeper

plugged to the hard-core,
picking along
the welted, stretchmarked
curve of the world.

Seamus Heaney

Dai Slate

Meet Dai, thirty-three years splitting
slate in a blue-grey
tomb beneath the
blue-grey town.

Drilled like a
colander,
rammed with a
thousand charges of
pitch and gunpowder,
wadded and tamped with
paper and dust by the
brass stamping rod, he
endured an eternal
winter of dull blasts
loosening great
slabs from the pillar of
himself.

He broke along the line of
cleavage. In the
long night's dripping
damp he had grown so
blue and grey, he
fingermarked; so
flat and brittle, he would
chip at touch.

Crumbled, he lies here now
under his slate headstone,
nestling among the
marred hills and the
tips of slag, overlooking the
grey-blue, silk-smooth
lintels, sills and
clothesline posts.

In the often rain, the
bare bulbs of the
street lamps turn the
roofs black satin.

Dora Polk

23

Mendin' Boots

The smell of laburnum comes as though along
The air; I sit in the high room, my fingers poised
Above the white blank paper, miles from where
The place is, but still it comes until
Firmly at last he sits beneath the cupboard—
The musty hole in which I hid and thought
A tunnel reaching to the sky—mendin' boots.
Sun streams along the table through the green
Glass of the lamp, illuminates a huge
Refracted wick. I watch, feeling his strength,
His taught fingers working, folded round
The cold iron as he twists the pincers, ripping
Old leather, steel claws. I smell the loosed
Dust roll along the air like flecks of gold
Where the boot, held hard against his thin chest,
Seems grown to bone. Later, on the last,
I hear the sharp tack, as one by one, the sprigs
Sink with the abrupt hammer blows
Into the brown smooth surface of the sole.
I hear the rasp scrape away edges,
Smell the wax as his wrists work round and round,
For mendin' boots is all skill, they are
Hob-nailed and clean beside the candlewick
Which smokes now. I see him sit back with gleaming
Eyes and smell his hair, his breath come through
The years, like fire over darkening hills.
I feel the satisfaction there, in the slow
Heart's beat beneath my heart, and the silence,
For mendin' boots is all skill. From the mine
He would come, worn and pale in his baggy trews,
His body slumped in the soft chair, waiting
For boots to wear thin that for an instant like
A king he might preside, resplendent, proud above
The dominion of a boot or a shoe, but the image
Blurs, the room floods back, table, chair
And book in the silence stare. Outside I hear
The sound of tugs, and the long drone of night.
In a directionless place I sit solitary, and alone,
Watching the darkness come, filling my mouth,
And my eyes until, embracing nothing, I rise
Lazarus-like and find you warm, and alive.

Evan Gwyn Williams

24

Chinese Acrobats

There are no drums, no fanfares
Not even a tremor of tambour
For art is all, needs no accompaniment.
Simplicity the keynote
Puff of white cloud stands backcloth
Rides a wide waste of sky.

Nothing to distract. The acrobats
Move on velvet feet, each
Deliberate action poised, considered.
They climb, grow outward as a tree
Swing, spin, amaze by sheer agility
And grace of limb.

There is beauty, humour
In performance. Whirling discs
Create design, pattern in flower-form
A frieze frozen in air.
Breaking the spell of spun plates tossed across
A juggler bows ironically, mocks at
Another's skill. Cooks cheerful
In a bare kitchen prop eggs atop
Produce a flutter of scared bird
From the terminal shell.

Their acts argue
Against probability, are in theory
Inpracticable. Yet exist beyond belief.
The acrobats obedient
In a controlled sphere handle
China pots, plates, parasols
The whole paraphernalia
Of sophisticated art
—And even final applause, praise—
Artlessly as pleased children.

M. A. B. Jones

Vital

I think my work is important, I am a link
In a long chain.
I had to have the training for it,
And I had to dirty my hands.
They ask my advice when they want to know
    what would be best.
I might move up even higher, in time.

On Sunday, I woke up shouting. She said,
What on earth's the matter, we're supposed to be
Going out to dinner later; or rather lunch.
I dressed, and played with Lynda, and
Felt a bit better.

I was called into the office from the shop
Floor. 'Mr Fletton, up from London, wants to see you.'
But I was hearing the mutter-mutter,
The kind-of giggling noises inside the machines
Through four thick concrete walls.
I could not read the words in front of my eyes.

She said last Thursday, you haven't said a thing
The whole evening.
I said no. I've been watching.
. . . I couldn't name a thing I'd seen on the screen.

Today is vital, people are relying on me
To get ten thousand packages out on time.
I am part of a chain, a link, they ask my advice.
I open the front door. After the wind,
It's a lovely cool morning, and sun;
Very bright.
The keys of the Toledo are clenched wet
In my right hand. And I don't move.
I am standing shaking. I am standing, shaking.

Alan Brownjohn

26

Executive

I am a young executive. No cuffs than mine are cleaner;
I have a Slimline briefcase and I use the firm's Cortina.
In every roadside hostelry from here to Burgess Hill
The *maîtres d'hôtel* all know me well and let me sign the bill.

You ask me what it is I do. Well actually, you know,
I'm partly a liaison man and partly P.R.O.
Essentially I integrate the current export drive
And basically I'm viable from ten o'clock till five.

For vital off-the-record work—that's talking transport-wise—
I've a scarlet Aston-Martin—and does she go? She flies!
Pedestrians and dogs and cats—we mark them down for slaughter.
I also own a speed-boat which has never touched the water.

She's built of fibre-glass, of course. I call her 'Mandy Jane'
After a bird I used to know—No soda, please, just plain—
And how did I acquire her? Well to tell you about that
And to put you in the picture I must wear my other hat.

I do some mild developing. The sort of place I need
Is a quiet country market town that's rather run to seed.
A luncheon and a drink or two, a little *savoir faire*—
I fix the Planning Officer, the Town Clerk and the Mayor.

And if some preservationist attempts to interfere
A 'dangerous structure' notice from the Borough Engineer
Will settle any buildings that are standing in our way—
The modern style, sir, with respect, has really come to stay.

John Betjeman

Swineherd

'When all this is over', said the swineherd,
'I mean to retire, where
Nobody will have heard about my special skills
And conversation is mainly about the weather.

I intend to learn how to make coffee, at least as well
As the Portuguese lay-sister in the kitchen
And polish the brass fenders every day.
I want to lie awake at night
Listening to cream crawling to the top of the jug
And the water lying soft in the cistern.

I want to see an orchard where the trees grow in straight lines
And the yellow fox finds shelter between the navy-blue trunks,
Where it gets dark early in summer
And the apple-blossom is allowed to wither on the bough.'

Eiléan Ní Chuilleanáin

Owen Has Retired

He was a hewer of coal.
There was no alternative.
Cot and school filled time
Between birth and work.
At the sound of hooter
He rose for Cynon Pit to share
With comrades the continuous
Dark, the certain dangers.

A master of rock and timber
He laboured half a century
In semi-darkness, hooking
And slinging coal in places
Less than table high.

Now under a safe sky
He potters, forgets the date
And to remove his cap.
Cynon Pit smokes
And rattles close by
But Owen neither looks
Nor listens, for he's earned
His proud nonchalance.

Robert Morgan

Cold Song

The doctor gazed
at the sack of guts passing
and saw
my pretty girl.

The lawyer looked at
a ringless finger
and saw my
pretty girl.

The professor noticed
eyes quick with intelligence
and
saw my pretty girl.

I met my pretty girl
and saw an intelligent
sack of guts with
a ringless finger.

Norman MacCaig

Park Note

Disgusted by the weight of his own sorrow
I saw one evening
a stranger open wide his coat
and taking out from under it his heart
throw the thing away.

Away over the railings, out across the parks,
across the lakes and the grasses,
as if after much confusion
he had decided not to care but

to move on lightly, carelessly,
amazed and with a grin upon his face
that seemed to say, 'Absurd
how easy that was done.'

Brian Patten

Society

Unauthorized Persons, including Poets, Strictly Prohibited

Dear Clare, you really would go mad
if you could come back now
to your own country. Your
favourite woods are completely gone
and the spinneys protected by guard-dogs.

You would find it a strange landscape
with arrogant signs jabbing
at eyeballs—'Keep Out',
'Beware of Alsations', 'Unauthorized
Persons Strictly Prohibited'.

Yes, and that includes poets,
anyone in fact who would
like to walk through a field
or search near the roots of a hedge
for the season's first primrose.

You remember Swordy Well, Royce Woods
and Helpston Heath? Then remember,
for they exist now only in the memory
and in the bright words picked by you
one morning when no-one was looking.

Edward Storey

30

Address to a Head of State

I am approaching you, our President, as a great
    Father figure who has given us
All we have, armed police by day and secret police
    By night. Everything is based on fear
As it should be, with a little bribery and
    Corruption thrown in. Although
Political trials have not yet been abolished
    We have the deep satisfaction of
Knowing that the most brutal forms of state repression
    Are, for the moment at least, in
Abeyance. Some of us are sent down the salt mines
    But we have the happy feeling that
There is always a lower rung under the feet
    Of every citizen on the ladder
Of state for still more unworthy men and women.
    The prerequisite for advancement
Or even for the retention of one's present post
    Is a routine agreement to lie
To oneself, to betray one's friends and to deceive
    One's masters. This leads to apathy,
To the acceptance of the present admirable
    Situation. I appeal to you, Mr President,
Never to let in the intellectuals, the artists,
    Who must continue to live and enjoy
A clandestine existence, cut off from every
    Possibility of polluting
Our beautifully instructed minds and hearts.
    So-called art: Poems, plays, novels, films,
May have been lost but what does that matter compared with
    The deepening of our confidence
In the irrepressible growth of our public image.
    Order pervades everything and for this
We have to thank you, the author of our well-being.
    Standards are rising and history
That can always be rewritten is on our side.
    We bow to your superior knowledge
And the monolithic grandeur of your great regime.
    Finally I beg to submit to you
A proposal that I should be promoted to a
    Higher post in order to maintain
The precision of our faultless state machinery.

Ronald Bottrall

Skyjack

Gun-toting men guard doors,
Gangways and exits of an innocent plane.
No more the mind is filled with business, holiday.
The purposed journey fails.

Terror takes over. Passengers,
Pilots in encapsulated seats
Cannot speak out. Fear has become
Companion alone, too close for confidence.

Travellers in a maze of glassed-in
Corridor watch distantly. Drama takes shape
Upon the airport apron. Suddenly
Drab truth appals. A body slumps, is flung

Flat to the tarmac, crumples in full sight
Of all obsessed spectators. Faces trapped
Freeze at the window. What is now the fate
Of those unfortunates who are within
Cannot be reckoned by a reasoned guess.
The unknown threatens—the last loneliness.

M. A. B. Jones

Back from Australia

Cocooned in Time, at this inhuman height,
    The packaged food tastes neutrally of clay.
    We never seem to catch the running day
But travel on in everlasting night
With all the chic accoutrements of flight:
    Lotions and essences in neat array
    And yet another plastic cup and tray.
'Thank you *so* much. Oh no, I'm quite all right'.

At home in Cornwall hurrying autumn skies
    Leave Bray Hill barren, Stepper jutting bare,
        And hold the moon above the sea-wet sand.
The very last of late September dies
    In frosty silence and the hills declare
        How vast the sky is looked at from the land.

John Betjeman

32

Tourist Promotion

For the tourists, who stay in the
Large new tourist hotels, the
Chief tourist attractions are the
Other large new tourist hotels.

For the querulous and wayward
There were once the local monkeys,
Who lived in the ancient tree-tops
Long before the hotels were thought of.
The tourists enticed the monkeys down
From the trees with monkey nuts and
Breakfast rolls. And the monkeys
Scampered across the road and were
Squashed by the buses transporting
Fresh tourists to see the monkeys.
It was not a pretty sight.

So now the tourists are confined to
The tourist hotels, large and new.
They pass with the greatest of ease
From one to the other, escorted by porters
With large new umbrellas, or even through
Underground passages, air-conditioned and
Adorned with murals by local artists,
Conveying impressions of the local scene.
After all, the tourist hotels were created
Specifically for the sake of the tourists.

D. J. Enright

Crowle, Tibberton, etc.

Not quite dormitory villages yet but will be
soon. The houses that remain from older days, from
the original village, are set athwart or
sideways from the road, or down a track. There's
reason for these irregularities that
the new bungalows do not comprehend—they

are all set so straight, wide-windowed
to the scene of verge and brick and chimney-piece
that brought them here and that they may yet
destroy. For an old inhabitant dies, the land's
sold, the cottage quietly demolished and
another new bungalow goes up. The foundations differ.
No one queries that. It is straight, it has
no unnecessary corners, is in keeping with
all those other bungalows. They'll soon create
another village of their own.

                    For the moment,
the oddities remain. The paths led and lead still
to still-used pasturage, the crooked cottage
was thus set for access to that crowded orchard
that still lies behind, the little house out of the true
was church property and brought in profitable
peppercorn rent from that odd-shaped piece of land.
And the gardens, the more they are grown, the more
they respond, richer and richer from loam of generations
of old flowers dug in, mulched to make good soil
for their popular pansies and geraniums. And
in each cottage lives a family that makes
its livelihood from farms around, whose members
set out on bikes, on damp mornings, raincoats
belted with string, and leave but little mark upon
the road. Nevertheless, they belong to the land.
The finned and spectacular cars from the bungalows
leave muddy swerves on the verge and in the lane.

The bungalow gardens dry out too quickly.
They need time. They are too regular, too bare.
Their new owners want instant growth and haven't
the patience of the countrymen; so, because they will not
accept that all gardens need shadowy corners
so that monkshood, sweet william, columbines
may grow, they plant the odd weeping willow
that grows quickly, the almost-instant evergreens,
the solitary lilac aesthetically placed and soon
flowering; these will not provide the necessary
richness for many years though. If they'd only
listen. 'Bushes along the house are often the best.'
'Oh no, that would encourage damp and harbour slugs!'
So out go gypsy rose and flowering currant and honeysuckle.

The old speak with the new, nod politely, but do not
consider them villagers yet. They, like their gardens,
need time and have years to go—if they do not
crowd out the old and take over. No one's thought of that
yet.

On June evenings, the white-shirt-sleeved executive,
mowing his tidy-outlined lawn with the latest
power machine, pauses occasionally, wishes to make
conversation with his neighbour but feels—
no, not excluded nor rebuffed—unnecessarily garrulous.
For the old fellow next door, a grunt's enough,
friendly but not for making conversation, that's not
his line. He grins and that's as good. His bald head
shines, he is uncollared, his sleeves are rolled
right to his shoulder line. The day's stubble of beard
gleams in the last rays of the sun. A man at his ease.
He stoops among his spuds, listens to the bees so busy
among his snapdragons. Certainly he never expects to be
moved on or out. He straightens a moment, looks around.
His black unpedigreed lurcher lies on the broken path,
snapping at flies—the path will not be mended
until someone complains; it serves the clothes line
and the vegetable plot quite adequately, leading from
the low dark door into the full garden. Nor do the height
and darkness of the cottage worry him—he only needs
light to read the newspaper by day and his wife
sits by the door to do her mending. He lights the lamp
when day is really done.

                    He glances next door before
he takes his coat from the clothes post, to go in;
he looks at the serried dazzle of windows quizzically,
and the wide doors. He thinks: plenty enough
fresh air outside for any man who cares to step
beyond his door. What's the point of all that glass,
losing warm air as well as comfort? He nods
at his neighbour (the townsman who will never be
a countryman but may possess, in time, with his like,
these homes, or places that were these homes) and steps
inside to the low warm fug, his dog at his heels.

Molly Holden

35

the young have left

the young have left
a place propped up on the frail
bones of pensioners.
crofts die under docken thistles nettles and
the absence of livestock.

jack, the youngest tenant, crouching into middle age, reads
history and the 'farming news' and keeps
his seven acres green.

elsewhere 'bed and breakfast' signs
invite the traveller to share
a traditional croft cuisine
bought from liptons mobile shop.
small gardens, bordered lawned and free from
hoofmarks, are hedged to hide
the wilderness beyond.

toward the sgeir, the house where andrew lived
is empty
mary peggy's roof has fallen in.

Angus Nicolson

Terminal Disease, Long Sutton

To look on the bright side, you could say
(Which is true) there will be more air;
More sun where there used to be shade; views
No-one has seen before.
But I do not like the sound of the saw
And would not choose
This view of a neighbour's pants and concrete
Sheds; the landing-lights on Odiham airfield.

And though, in theory,
Most of us now have wood
To last ten winters,
These logs aren't easy
To get going. (Take five fire-lighters,
Half a ton of kindling . . .)
They hiss, release black smoke, but
Do not actually burn.

36

Were our elms really dead, that had so much sap in them?
Where will our rooks build now?

Replanting hardwoods will take time; energy; money.
Nobody has any.
And the business of replanting—
Whose is it, exactly?
'The council ought . . .'
'What is the C.P.R.E. there for?'
'We're an elm landscape. We deserve
A government grant . . .'

We have already lost
The elm that served as village notice board;
Five trees by Chaffers' Close—and worse,
The group that proved (May till the end of August)
A natural boundary to the cricket field.
Our elms were huge. Their going throws the church,
The primary school, the rash of yellow, new-
Built bungalows into a harsh relief
That was not meant.
We have already lost an indigenous
Sense of proportion.

Someone must plant soon
Or we shall have left
Only the churchyard yews
Which have stood for a thousand years,
But which suddenly
Look sickly—

And fruit trees in the gardens:
Apple mostly;
A few cherry: pink; double-flowering; not the fruiting sort;
A plum or two;
The odd fig.

Is there a cure
For apathy? Could we inject
Against it?

Georgina Hammick

37

Gladstone Street

It was the place to go in nineteen-thirty,
And so we went. A housemaid or two
Still lingered on at the bigger houses.
A miner and his family were the next
To follow us there, had scarcely settled in
When the wife began dying, whitely visible
Through the bay window in their double bed.
At the back, the garden vanished
Under grass and a ramshackle shed.
People were sure the street was going downhill.
It literally was: cracks in our hall
Opened as the house started to subside
Towards the mines beneath. Miners were everywhere
Under that cancerous hill. My mother swore
That you could hear them tapping away below
Of a quiet night. Miners unnerved her so
Ever since one sat beside her on the train
And soiled her with his pit dirt. But it wasn't miners
Undid the street. The housemaids lasted
Until the war, then fed the factories.
Flat-dwellers came and went, in the divided houses,
Mothers unwedded who couldn't pay their rent.
A race of gardeners died, and a generation
Hacked down the walls to park their cars
Where the flowers once were. It was there it showed,
The feeble-minded style of the neighbourhood
Gone gaudily mad in painted corrugations,
Botches of sad carpentry. The street front has scarcely changed.
No one has recorded the place.
Perhaps we shall become sociology. We have outpaced
Gladstone's century. We might have been novels.

Charles Tomlinson

Outside

The towered church squats
among willows, dead elms and lindens
beside a deep pond nearly hid
in nettles, thistles, knapweed and briars.
The churchyard is bowered in weeds.

In one of its lost graves four children,
Belinda, Jane, Ivy and Tom
have lain more than a century.
Wild fairy flax is now their host.

The churchyard gate won't open.
How did those boys last week
find the place, climb the tower,
hurl a stone block down
on Belinda, Ivy, Tom and Jane,
push over an acanthus urn
which showed above uncut grass?
Did the pond's echo and the neglect of the place
make them so spurn reason?

If this was not so, one can't quite think
why the boys slashed the unused altar,
broke a vase. No theft: moneyed pockets coveted nothing . . .
I cannot hate those heirs of our violence
our vandals. (Though no doubt I might
if I came face to face with them here.)
The church is locked, the altar flat.
Is it the boys, or we, who are shut out?
Or could it possibly be God? And from what?

Anne Tibble

Glasgow 5 March 1971

With a ragged diamond
of shattered plate-glass
a young man and his girl
are falling backwards into a shop-window.
The young man's face
is bristling with fragments of glass
and the girl's leg has caught
on the broken window
and spurts arterial blood
over her wet-look white coat.
Their arms are starfished out
braced for impact,
their faces show surprise, shock,
and the beginning of pain.

39

The two youths who have pushed them
are about to complete the operation
reaching into the window
to loot what they can smartly.
Their faces show no expression.
It is a sharp clear night
in Sauchiehall Street.
In the background two drivers
keep their eyes on the road.

Edwin Morgan

The Victim Died of Stab Wounds

It was when the novelty of life
Wore off he bought a flick-knife;
And the leather jacket he stole
Because it was a status symbol
That helped him to play it cool,
To prove he was nobody's fool.

Then he ganged up. He was only
Doing what insecure, lonely
Types do, as the psychiatrist
Pointed out. Put to the test,
He had no option but to climb
The ladder of petty crime.

What's more vulnerable than age?
A man counting dough in his dotage,
Before the shop door shuts,
Asks for it. But it takes guts
To grab the loot and scarper
Under the busy nose of a copper.

You don't expect old men to show
Fight, to bellow, to blow
A referee's whistle. It's a life
For a life. The flick-knife
Burns in the sweating palm
Of the hand that means no harm.

It's that simple. As for death,
What is it? You buy a wreath,
Pull down a blind, drink a pint
In memory of some old skinflint,
Then put it out of your mind
Until you next pull down a blind.

A death is a natural thing. A killing
Is a special sort of thing.
The slob had let him down by dying;
He lay there not even trying
To live. The flick-knife stuck
Out of him. What bloody luck!

It's the enormity of the offence
Proves, in a way, its innocence.
Not that this helped him much
Before the Bench. He lost touch
Somehow with himself. Disgrace
Stamped on a magistrate's face

Didn't register. What maybe did
Was the shock of the blood
Trickling slowly into a crack.
If he could, he would have put it back
Into the body. That he never can
Makes him, prematurely, a man.

F. Pratt Green

The Sounds Begin Again

The sounds begin again;
the siren in the night
the thunder at the door
the shriek of nerves in pain.

Then the keening crescendo
of faces split by pain
the wordless, endless wail
only the unfree know.

41

Importunate as rain
the wraiths exhale their woe
over the sirens, knuckles, boots;
my sounds begin again.

Dennis Brutus

Open Day at Porton

These bottles are being filled with madness,
A kind of liquid madness concentrate
Which can be drooled across the land
Leaving behind a shuddering human highway . . .

A welder trying to eat his arm.

Children pushing stale food into their eyes
To try to stop the chemical spectaculars
Pulsating inside their hardening skulls.

A health visitor throwing herself downstairs,
Climbing the stairs, throwing herself down again
Shouting: Take the nails out of my head.

There is no damage to property.

Now, nobody likes manufacturing madness,
But if we didn't make madness in bottles
We wouldn't know how to deal with bottled madness.

We don't know how to deal with bottled madness.

We all really hate manufacturing madness
But if we didn't make madness in bottles
We wouldn't know how to be sane.

Responsible madness experts assure us
Britain would never be the first
To uncork such a global brainquake.

But suppose some foreign nut sprayed Kent
With his insanity aerosol . . .
Well, there's only one answer to madness.

Adrian Mitchell

New Town Blues

I. Culture

Near half a week's pay on the blonde bouffant
and a pair of thigh length boots,
she queens the fore-court
to lighten many a darkness.
A workman, pasting posters
for the town's Arts Festival,
draws breath at the callipygian exposé
as she bends to remove a petrol cap.
He is not one for minority pursuits.
She thinks of what to get the kids for tea.

II. Environment

Grandma constantly tells how, as a girl,
she held the horses in the fields,
wiped them down at the end of the day
and slept by them in the stable.
While her grandson,
cut off by regiments of streets
and a technology that ostracises him,
each Saturday on the way back from the pub
kicks in the bus-shelter to show them.
And they, as regularly, repair it in reply.

III. Social Services

At the shopping centre they sit on benches,
a refuge from a hostile domesticity.
Grey stubble above grubby neckbands,
redolent of pipes and weak bladders,
they fumble for matches with thickly veined hands
while they soak in the last of the summer.
Memories revived by the young wives
with their sturdy hams, they recall places
the authorities considered unsuitable.

John Cotton

Pagans

On the Housing Estate
it's great,
radio and television,
lollipops and misprision,
and Eve talking
to the insurance man at the gate.

Here the lucky Pair
have given the go-by to God,
they don't even know they are bare,
nor have heard of the iron rod.

They have escaped the eye
of watchful Deity,
given the go-by
to holy Theology,
quite innocently, not knowing
their dues, or duties, or
which way the wind's blowing.

No light in the sky,
no rumbling Word,
no telecast Eye,
at the gate, no sword.

Childlike and simple and free,
they have skipped the sermon and come
for telly and kippers and tea,
to their subsidized heavenly home.

Arthur Bull

Glasgow Sonnet

A mean wind wanders through the backcourt trash.
Hackles on puddles rise, old mattresses
puff briefly and subside. Play-fortresses
of brick and bric-a-brac spill out some ash.
Four storeys have no windows left to smash,
but in the fifth a chipped sill buttresses
mother and daughter the last mistresses

of that black block condemned to stand, not crash.
Around them the cracks deepen, the rats crawl.
The kettle whimpers on a crazy hob.
Roses of mould grow from ceiling to wall.
The man lies late since he has lost his job,
smokes on one elbow, letting his coughs fall
thinly into an air too poor to rob.

Edwin Morgan

Neighbour, Tenth Floor

Beyond a span of wall
        I can imagine you:

gaping
        your sleep-soured dawnbreaths,
waking
        your habitual body,
and in a web of bedclothes
sitting up
        dishevelled
to grope for clock and eyeglasses
as I reach out for mine.

I know you pace your cage,
halfway up to the sky
in this communal ivory tower,
for I hear your footsteps
echoing mine
        in the adjacent cell.

When you flush your waste
my cistern gurgles too,
and the mutter of my saucepans
answers the descant of yours.

Boxed in our hired cubicles
we act the self-same ings
feeding cursing waiting
and watching television
(that disingenuous window).

We nod civilly on thresholds,
grin cosily in liftcars,
and disappear
scuttling like land-crabs
into separate occasions.

Daily I want to rush to you
weeping with recognition
and embrace you calling,
calling,
>   I am your neighbour
>   Love me,

then live with you,
together away
>   from these lonely dens;

but what would be the use?

It is better to tap out an endless message
against that imperceptible wall
that must always divide us.

A. L. Hendriks

The Mayflower

The Fathers set sail
with a load of sin,
with a cargo of care,
from here to there.

Rollin' an pukin' an pitchin'
over Atlantic Hell's kitchen.

Carried saws and axes and spades,
nails in plenty, and wives, and maids,
horse-shoes and bacon,
flour and cheese,
by wind and wave, through sightless seas:
with bag and baggage, box and chest,
down in the hold, deep in the dark,
they packed a peck of trouble,
in their rolling Ark.

46

And tucked away, in the deepest spot,
below the hardware and corn and seed,
in the secretest silence, quite forgot,
lay a box that plainly said, on the lid,
Not wanted on voyage, and no kid.

Not wanted on voyage it said, no more,—
but when they came to the promised shore,
to the Land where sin should be forbid,
where the righteous should reign, far from
    bishop and king,
on the strand of hope, the new domain,
the box was opened,—and out flew, what?

Gangsters and murder, drugs and drink,
the wreckage of innocence, there on the brink,—
on the sands of the Bay, a monster got out,
and Comus was there, with all his rout.
In vain the Ark, the sundering seas,
Sin and the Devil had sailed aboard,
the mighty pair, and landfall made,
in this bright New World, to loll at ease,
as once in an older Garden's shade!

Arthur Bull

Religion

Nobbut God

'First on, there was nobbut God.'
Genesis, *Chap. 1, v.1. Yorkshire Dialect Translation.*

First on
There was silence.
And God said:
'Let there be clatter.'

The wind, unclenching,
Runs its thumbs
Along dry bristles of Yorkshire Fog.

The mountain ousel
Oboes its one note.

After rain
Water lobelia
Drips like a tap
On the tarn's tight surface-tension.

But louder,
And every second nearer,
Like chain explosions
From furthest nebulae
Light-yearing across space:
The thudding of my own blood.

'It's nobbut me,'
Says God.

Norman Nicholson

Creation

God did not write:
He spoke.
He made.
His jack-knife had a superblade.
He sliced the earth
And carved the water,
Made man and woman
By an act of slaughter.

He scattered polished diamonds
In the sky—like dust—
And gave the world a push to set it spinning.
What super-deity got him beginning,
Whispered in his ear on how to do it
Gave hints on what was to be done?

Don't ask.
In his mouth he felt the sun
Spat it out because it burned;
From between his toes—the moon—
He could not walk so kicked it free.
His work was finished.
He put a river round his neck,
And vanished.

Alan Sillitoe

Finis

The Power behind said to God:

This creature You have made,
is a bit of a bungled job.

You have taken four billion years,
or five,
to produce a model
notable chiefly for its
tendency to quarrel and fight,
and swive:
it kills almost on sight,

makes Laws, on tables of stone,
and breaks them one by one.

We think you had better with a flick
and swish of cosmic dust propel
this creature to annihilation, or hell,—

Cancel the contract You made
with Adam or Abraham,
or some such name,
rule off, and try again.

God made a sign
of contrition
to the Other,
and drew the requested line.

Arthur Bull

The Coming

And God held in his hand
A small globe. Look, he said.
The son looked. Far off,
As through water, he saw
A scorched land of fierce
Colour. The light burned
There; crusted buildings
Cast their shadows; a bright
Serpent, a river
Uncoiled itself, radiant
With slime.
        On a bare
Hill a bare tree saddened
The sky. Many people
Held out their thin arms
To it, as though waiting
For a vanished April
To return to its crossed
Boughs. The son watched
Them. Let me go there, he said.

R. S. Thomas

Never Again

You never saw such a stupid mess,
The government, of course, were to blame.
That poor young kid in her shabby dress
And the old chap with her, it seemed such a shame.

She had the baby in a backyard shed,
It wasn't very nice, but the best we could do.
Just fancy, a manger for a bed,
I ask you, what's the world coming to?

We're sorry they had to have it so rough,
But we had our troubles, too, remember,
As if all the crowds were not enough
The weather was upside-down for December.

There was singing everywhere, lights in the sky
And those drunken shepherds neglecting their sheep
And three weird foreigners in full cry—
You just couldn't get a good night's sleep.

Well now they've gone, we can all settle down,
There's room at the inn and the streets are so still
And we're back to normal in our own little town
That nobody's heard of, or ever will.

And though the world's full of people like those,
I think of them sometimes, especially her,
And one can't help wondering . . . though I don't suppose
Anyone will ever know who they were.

Harri Webb

Song for a Winter Birth

Under the watchful lights
    A child was born;
From a mortal house of flesh
    Painfully torn.

51

And we, who later assembled
  To praise or peer,
Saw merely an infant boy
  Sleeping there.

Then he awoke and stretched
  Small arms wide
And for food or comfort
  Quavering cried.

A cry and attitude
  Rehearsing in small
The deathless death still haunting
  The Place of the Skull.

Outside, in the festive air,
  We lit cigars.
The night was nailed to the sky
  With hard bright stars.

Vernon Scannell

Small Wire

My faith
is a great weight
hung on a small wire,
as doth the spider
hang her baby on a thin web,
as doth the vine,
twiggy and wooden,
hold up grapes
like eyeballs,
as many angels
dance on the head of a pin.

God does not need
too much wire to keep Him there,
just a thin vein,
with blood pushing back and forth in it,
and some love.

As it has been said:
Love and a cough
cannot be concealed.
Even a small cough.
Even a small love.
So if you have only a thin wire,
God does not mind.
He will enter your hands
as easily as tens cents used to
bring forth a Coke.

Anne Sexton

My Believing Bones

Swung by the rhythm of
a yes and no
between the living and
the dead I go.
The dance is in my bones
and though I see
that every dancing bone
will cease to be
I will believe my bones
and learn to trust
my living and my dying,
for I must.

Coming and going by
the dance, I see
that what I am not is
a part of me.
Dancing is all that I
can ever trust,
the dance is all I am,
the rest is dust.
I will believe my bones
and live by what
will go on dancing when
my bones are not.

Sydney Carter

No Answer

But the chemicals in
My mind were not
Ready, so I let
Him go on, dissolving
The word on my
Tongue. Friend, I had said,
Life is too short for
Religion; it takes time
To prepare a sacrifice
For the God. Give yourself
To science that reveals
All, asking no pay
For it. Knowledge is power;
The old oracle
Has not changed. The nucleus
In the atom awaits
Our bidding. Come forth,
We cry, and the dust spreads
Its carpet. Over the creeds
And masterpieces our wheels go.

R. S. Thomas

Aldershot Crematorium

Between the swimming-pool and cricket-ground
  How straight the crematorium driveway lies!
And little puffs of smoke without a sound
  Show what we loved dissolving in the skies,
Dear hands and feet and laughter-lighted face
And silk that hinted at the body's grace.

But no-one seems to know quite what to say
  (Friends are so altered by the passing years):
'Well, anyhow, it's not so cold today'—
  And thus we try to dissipate our fears.
'I am the resurrection and the Life':
Strong, deep and painful, doubt inserts the knife.

John Betjeman

54

The Empty Church

They laid this stone trap
for him, enticing him with candles,
as though he would come like some huge moth
out of the darkness to beat there.
Ah, he had burned himself
before in the human flame
and escaped, leaving the reason
torn. He will not come any more

to our lure. Why, then, do I kneel still
striking my prayers on a stone
heart? Is it in hope one
of them will ignite yet and throw
on its illumined walls the shadow
of someone greater than I can understand?

R. S. Thomas

The Island

And God said, I will build a church here
And cause this people to worship me,
And afflict them with poverty and sickness
In return for centuries of hard work
And patience. And its walls shall be hard as
Their hearts, and its windows let in the light
Grudgingly, as their minds do, and the priest's words be drowned
By the wind's caterwauling. All this I will do,

Said God, and watch the bitterness in their eyes
Grow, and their lips suppurate with
Their prayers. And their women shall bring forth
On my altars, and I will choose the best
Of them to be thrown back into the sea.

And that was only on one island.

R. S. Thomas

Varieties of Religious Experience

Under the Bo-tree the Buddha sat
With his arms like this and his legs like that,
Achieving mystical exaltation
By inhibiting his circulation.

On top of old Smoky, in rotten weather,
Moses, at the end of his tether,
Was impressed by what he thought he heard,
Came rolling down the mountain with the Word.

To the sands of the desert the Prophet fled
Listening to noises inside his head,
Took down from dictation Allah's writ
While building up to a nasty fit.

While on the road to Damascus Paul
Seems to have had a most painful fall,
Was dazzled by the sun's hot glare
And saw a man who wasn't there.

He wasn't there again today
And now he'll never go away.
The moral of all this, dear brother,
Is: facts are one thing, truth another.

Harri Webb

Reformation

The hazed meadows of England grow over chancels
Where cattle hooves kick up heraldic tiles
And molehills heap their spoils above slumped walls.
The cruck-beamed roofs of refectories nestle under
Sheds and barns, hay piled high where
Augustine and Aquinas chapter by chapter
Were read in these now lapsed pastoral acres.

Small streams wash the smashed crockery of Cistercians.
Stone-plaited carvings are wedged in gable ends
Of farmhouses, springs irrigate robbed chapels
Where all is marsh, reeds meshed among cracked altars.
A buzzard shrieks *yaa-i* in a tall tree,
Plainchant echoing along the valleys.
High hedges stand above spoiled finials.

And Sunday mornings see small meeting houses,
Reformed parishes and tabernacles,
Bethesdas and the whole wide countryside,
All split seven ways in sect and congregation,
Assembling to praise God from whom all blessings
Flow through his derelict priories, abbeys, cells
The afternoon sun will show, faint shadows among fields.

Anthony Thwaite

Pollution

Going, Going

I thought it would last my time—
The sense that, beyond the town,
There would always be fields and farms,
Where the village louts could climb
Such trees as were not cut down;
I knew there'd be false alarms

In the papers about old streets
And split-level shopping, but some
Have always been left so far;
And when the old part retreats
As the bleak high-risers come
We can always escape in the car.

Things are tougher than we are, just
As earth will always respond
However we mess it about;
Chuck filth in the sea, if you must:
The tides will be clean beyond.
—But what do I feel now? Doubt?

Or age, simply? The crowd
Is young in the M1 café;
Their kids are screaming for more—
More houses, more parking allowed,
More caravan sites, more pay.
On the Business Page, a score

Of spectacled grins approve
Some takeover bid that entails

Five per cent profit (and ten
Per cent more in the estuaries): move
Your works to the unspoilt dales
(Grey area grants)! And when

You try to get near the sea
In summer . . .
                        It seems, just now,
To be happening so very fast;
Despite all the land left free
For the first time I feel somehow
That it isn't going to last,

That before I snuff it, the whole
Boiling will be bricked in
Except for the tourist parts—
First slum of Europe: a role
It won't be so hard to win,
With a cast of crooks and tarts.

And that will be England gone,
The shadows, the meadows, the lanes,
The guildhalls, the carved choirs.
There'll be books; it will linger on
In galleries; but all that remains
For us will be concrete and tyres.

Most things are never meant.
This won't be, most likely: but greeds
And garbage are too thick-strewn
To be swept up now, or invent
Excuses that make them all needs.
I just think it will happen, soon.

Philip Larkin

November Resort

Little bright boats lying idle in the tidal estuary.
The ghost of the locked, deserted funfair:
Remembered rides on the
                        Rollercoaster
Musing in the mist . . .

Caretakers of holiday camps tend the precious crops of caravans
Acre upon acre, like marrows,
And the dormant tents which will spring like toadstools
Out of the summer mornings.
The Bingo hall is broody as a hen,
Huddled in a hedge, and hatching
Batteries of fun for free-range visitors
Free-range fun for batteries of coach tours.
And all along the lonely shore
                              the rubbish tip
Is nearly level with the road.

Jean Williams

The Reservoir

The air shaken by booms, blasting charges
Vast detonations, echoes rumbling
This was our lot for months. In all these
Almost forgotten that earlier noise
Shock of losing our valley, explosions
In speech, print, questions in the House
The wasted protest marches. That battle lost
Now we must watch in sorrow the slow drift
Of natural life from the land.

Birds leave their nests, fly to further
Recesses of the wild hills. Badgers
Desert setts, Reynard now needs
No pack to root him out. There is
Unbelievable massacre
Of field mice, shrews, insects. Dust settles
As a blight on trees. Throughout hot summer
No butterflies are seen.

This winter, with work like our small rivers
In full spate, falling rock dislodged
By frost fingers will crash from heights.
There will be landslides, loose shale
In quagmires of clay. Spring will come
With more loud armament, piledrivers
Excavators, grotesque cranes. Stone
Concrete poured in will be rammed down

60

Create roots for the dam. A wall
Of masonry will grow, impacted firmly
In the valley throat. We know this.
We have seen it all before.

Later, looking at the broad lake
Filled to the brim, water limpid
Surface delicately flawed by sparks struck
Crystalline from evanescent sun
We shall forget past desolation.
We shall point out to strangers the place
Of lost landmarks. Conscious then
Of new beauty lapping innocent shores
We shall be proud of it. We know this too.

M. A. B. Jones

Delectable Duchy

Where yonder villa hogs the sea
Was open cliff to you and me.
The many-coloured cara's fill
The salty marsh to Shilla Mill.
And, foreground to the hanging wood,
Are toilets where the cattle stood.
The mint and meadowsweet would scent
The brambly lane by which we went;
Now, as we near the ocean roar,
A smell of deep-fry haunts the shore.
In pools beyond the reach of tides
The Senior Service carton glides,
And on the sand the surf-line lisps
With wrappings of potato crisps.
The breakers bring with merry noise
Tribute of broken plastic toys
And lichened spears of blackthorn glitter
With harvest of the August litter.
Here in the late October light
See Cornwall, a pathetic sight,
Raddled and put upon and tired
And looking somewhat over-hired,
Remembering in the autumn air
The years when she was young and fair—

Those golden and unpeopled bays,
The shadowy cliffs and sheep-worn ways,
The white unpopulated surf,
The thyme- and mushroom-scented turf,
The slate-hung farms, the oil-lit chapels,
Thin elms and lemon-coloured apples—
Going and gone beyond recall
Now she is free for 'One and All'.*

One day a tidal wave will break
Before the breakfasters awake
And sweep the cara's out to sea,
The oil, the tar, and you and me,
And leave in windy criss-cross motion
A waste of undulating ocean
With, jutting out, a second Scilly,
The isles of Roughtor and Brown Willy.

*The motto of Cornwall.

John Betjeman

Loss of an Oil Tanker

Over our heads the missiles ran
Through skies more desolate than the sea.
In jungles, where man hides from man,
Leaves fell, in springtime, from the tree.

A cracked ship on the Seven Stones lies
Dying in resurrection weather.
With squalid hands we hold our prize:
A drowned fish and a sea-bird's feather.

Charles Causley

Oil

With our eyes closed, our mouths open—
Our ears stuffed against the storm—
We slept secure enough;
Not knowing what God was sending.

62

To-day each wave is fringed
With the blue metallic sheen of oil.
Each strand of kelp bleeds blue
Back to the sea
And the footprints of the herring gull
Are edged in red and indigo.
On every pool a thin skin of blue and yellow
Mirrors sky.

God has been spitting oil
At Boggle Hole
Thick brown gobs of it
That smell like polish slick the rocks,
Discolour sand.

The tide's reach is a trail of death—
Of feather, fin and vertebrae.
The starfish lies, contused and broken,
In smithereens of crab and claw.

There was a time
We would have named this Devil's work
For coming in October; His month
When the brambling stopped
For the club
He laid across that shrub,
The mawk set inside the fruit.

The Devil no longer holds good. He
Was all in evil then
As God sat favoured in his sky—
Worshipped, feared, all-seeing.

As one has dropped from favour,
So's the other.
We now dismiss the devil's work—
Set all of that behind us.

An oil slick on the shore's
An Act of God
And the next tide takes away his dead.

Pete Morgan

Orkney

Out in the harbour gulls wheel
Swoop to the trough of an everlasting
Wave. Attitudes, patterns of islands
Satisfy. Smiles are not grudged
Where even the oceans are neighbourly
Atlantic nudging shoulders
With a cold North Sea.

In port the robust boat
Discharges its homely cargo.
Walking the quayside in a waiting time
You note old greystone houses rooted deep
In ripples, shoreline trapped
By ebb and flow of ancient history.

No one here aloof. All trustful, welcoming.
Old crafts, old ways, old rituals create
A simple life. Plain ideals stir
In cool and unpolluted air.
The uneventful landscape charms.
Land, sea preserve an antique harmony.

Offshore the oil-rigs anchor restlessly.

M. A. B. Jones

Tree

They didn't tell us
what it would be like
without trees.

Nobody imagined
that the whispering of leaves
would grow silent
or the vibrant jade of spring
pale to grey death.

And now we pile
rubbish on rubbish
in this dusty landscape—
struggling to create
        a tree

but though the shape is right
and the nailed branches
lean upon the wind
and plastic leaves
lend colour to the twigs

we wait in vain
for the slow unfurling of buds
and no amount of loving
can stir our weary tree
to singing.

Tina Morris

Throwing Trees

The executioners arrive.
In Hardy's time they used axes;
In my time they have mechanical saws.
Hardy's executioners were Job and Ike;
The two men I see are strangers.

The hum and purr continue
Through a long day's slaughter.
Most of the trees are sycamores
But all must go for the building
Of semi-detached bungalows.

They fall every four or five minutes
To the frenzy of piece-work.
At the end of the day the strangers
Swig beer, put on their jackets
And depart, proud of their work.

My kitchen window framed the little wood.
Now I see a gap and a plain field.
One hundred and forty trees have fallen!
When my children were small we walked
The paths and counted the trees.

Robert Morgan

Nature

Snow and Snow

Snow is sometimes a she, a soft one.
  Her kiss on your cheek, her finger on your sleeve
In early December, on a warm evening,
    And you turn to meet her, saying 'It's snowing!'
        But it is not. And nobody's there.
        Empty and calm is the air.

Sometimes the snow is a he, a sly one.
  Weakly he signs the dry stone with a damp spot.
Waifish he floats and touches the pond and is not.
    Treacherous-beggarly he falters, and taps at the window.
        A little longer he clings to the grass-blade tip
        Getting his grip.

Then how she leans, how furry foxwrap she nestles
  The sky with her warm, and the earth with her softness.
How her lit crowding fairytales sink through the space-silence
    To build her palace, till it twinkles in starlight—
        Too frail for a foot
        Or a crumb of soot.

Then how his muffled armies move in all night
  And we wake and every road is blockaded
Every hill taken and every farm occupied
  And the white glare of his tents is on the ceiling.
      And all that dull blue day and on into the gloaming
      We have to watch more coming.

Then everything in the rubbish-heaped world
  Is a bridesmaid at her miracle.

Dunghills and crumbly dark old barns are bowed in the chapel of her
sparkle,
The gruesome boggy cellars of the wood
Are a wedding of lace
Now taking place.

Ted Hughes

Spring She Says

Spring? (she says). A bit depressing at first,
beginning what one can't end:
all flighty blues and heady wind,
time zigzag, like a play of finches,—
capricious, too quick to hold.

Summer? A shapelier hammock; voluptuous, drowsy-rich,
the looped honeysuckle nostril-high,
the butterflies spread like painted fans,
time in a drift of dandelion . . .
over grass roots, everything.

Autumn making its own sadness, all
banners and castles down:
thistles in a rearguard longing,
mauve pyres of woodsmoke through the dusk . . .
time a theme on a 'cello, vast, dying.

And Winter? The air crisp, cold, suddenly
bright-cold, so sharply peeled;
children in their new berets
like holly, local, everlasting;
and time kindness, maybe a true beginning.

Geoffrey Holloway

Lives of the Poet

In Spring he saw the hedges splashed with blood;
Rags of flesh depended. In the moonlight
From a chestnut branch he saw suspended
A man who cocked an inattentive ear.

68

He heard worms salivate and paced his song
To the metronome of the hanging man,
Wore black to celebrate this time of year.

In August, from deceitful beaches, waves
Hauled drowners deeper in; he watched their arms
Wink in the obsolescent sun;
His ears discerned those other melodies
Beneath the chesty self-praise of the band,
The sound of blues. The shifting sand
And sea entombed clean bones, old summer days.

Now Autumn, vicar of all other weathers,
Performs its rites he joins the harvest chorus
At the cider-press and celebrates
In dance of words the seasons' grand alliance,
Puts on his snappiest suit on Friday nights
And stomps gay measures: no dirges now,
For Winter waits with ice and truth and silence.

Vernon Scannell

July the Seventh

Drugged all day, the summer
Flagged in its heat, brutal
Weather sullen as brass.
There was no comfort in darkness.
Hotter than breath we lay

On beds too warm for moving,
Near open windows. Full of
Spaces the house was, walls
Fretting for a brisk air.
A door slammed flat in its

Loud frame, banging us awake.
Wind was bringing in the storm.
Quick switches of whipped light
Flicked the rooftops, made shadowless
The ends of rooms. The stopped clock

69

Marked the lightning. I got up
Heavily, shut the house against
Thunder. Rain was a long time
Coming, then sparse drops, stinging
Like metal, hit the bricks, the hot

Pavements. When it sweetened
To plenty, the streets tamed it,
Flowed it in pipes and conduits,
Channelled it underground through
Stony runnels. The rain brought

So faint a smell of hay I searched
My mind for it, thinking it memory.
I lay freshly awake on the cool sheets,
Hearing the storm. Somewhere, far off,
Cut grass lay in files, the hay spoiling.

Leslie Norris

Lord Autumn

Lord Autumn's hair is the colour of foxes, his eyes
Burn like coals at Christmas, his hands
Strike sparks from the air as he runs.

Lord Autumn is all fire, and all on fire, his
Fingernails drip fire, his tongue darts forks
Of cold fire like a lizard, he carries
Tapers and torches, fed by the conflagration
Of his own flesh.

With a leap and a whoop Lord Autumn assumes the green wood.
He thrusts wildfire into the leaves. He rules among
Orchards and ruins.

Robert Nye

The Buzzard

The buzzard turns a circle in the sky,
making its ends meet.
When it completes the figure
a round blue segment drops out of the air
leaving a black hole
through which the souls of many little birds
fly up to heaven.

Alasdair Maclean

The Peregrine

His working eye has seen me
long before my leisure one sees him.
He straddles acres, treading air,
and sifts the turning world below
through meshes beetle-fine.

Computerized by evolution
he calculates the angle of the sun and wind
and the flight-path of a pigeon.
He adds them up
and finds the answer underneath.

Man sows his fields with poison now
and death works up the scale as well as down.
It isn't prey
this falcon bears so lightly off
but a Trojan Horse.

Alasdair Maclean

Owls

The owls are flying. From hedge to hedge
Their deep-mouthed voices call the fields
Of England, stretching north and north,
To a sibilant hunt above ditches;
And small crawlers, bent in crevices, yield
Juice of their threaded veins, with

A small kernel of bones. It was earlier
I walked the lace of the sea at this south
Edge, walked froths of the fallen moon
Bare-legged in the autumn water
So cold it set my feet like stones
In its inches, and I feel on breath

And ankles the touch of the charged sea
Since. I saw in my lifting eyes the flat
Of this one country, north stretching,
And north. I saw its hills, the public light
Of its cities, and every blatant tree
Burning, with assembled autumn burning.

I know the same sun, in a turn
Of earth, will bring morning, grey
As gulls or mice to us. And I know
In my troubled night the owls fly
Over us, wings wide as England,
And their voices will never go away.

Leslie Norris

The circle

Blackbirds are singing, the country over,
each in his own bud-clotted plot of land,
from central tree or roof or chimney-stack.
Each singing bird defies his singing neighbour:
this is my territory, these my lawns. Keep out.

It's a beautiful belligerence that rarely comes to blows.
Sometimes, clashing on the edge of territories,
they rise in twinkling combat (but without touch,
more ballet than battle) like black stars of the day,
and sink, and sing once more, and all
seems purely local.

          Yet—come to think of it—
each bird hears probably three others, and they
three more. And so the circle spreads and
—to be metaphysical—one might say that
in the spirit, if not in the voice, each bird
hears every other blackbird in the land
and so the bird who shouts on the outskirts
of Stirling hears and is defying and replying to
the sweet carollings of blackbirds in Somerset.

Molly Holden

Sparrow

He's no artist.
His taste in clothes is more
dowdy than gaudy.
And his nest—that blackbird, writing
pretty scrolls on the air with the gold nib of his beak,
would call it a slum.

To stalk solitary on lawns,
to sing solitary in midnight trees,
to glide solitary over grey Atlantics—
not for him: he'd rather
a punch-up in a gutter.

He carries what learning he has
lightly—it is, in fact, based only
on the usefulness whose result
is survival. A proletarian bird.
No scholar.

But when winter soft-shoes in
and these other birds—
ballet dancers, musicians, architects—
die in the snow
and freeze to branches,
watch him happily flying
on the O-levels and A-levels
of the air.

Norman MacCaig

Commotion

A trouble of rooks, cawing and jangling,
soaring and floating, side-flighting,
upsetting the sky; brawling and brangling,
some squawking credo of hate reciting,
as if old Nature, full of spite and rage,
jealous of our fair lawns and well-kept drives,
would cast, not dead leaves only, to assuage
her malice, but these feather-loose, footloose phantoms,
to vex us, with their ill-assorted lives.

Arthur Bull

Swifts

Fifteenth of May. Cherry blossom. The swifts
Materialize at the tip of a long scream
Of needle—'Look! They're back! Look!' And they're
    gone
On a steep

Controlled scream of skid
Round the house-end and away under the cherries.
    Gone.
Suddenly flickering in sky summit, three or four
    together,
Gnat-wisp frail, and hover-searching, and listening

For air-chills—are they too early? With a bowing
Power-thrust to left, then to right, then a flicker they
Tilt into a slide, a tremble for balance,
Then a lashing down disappearance

Behind elms.
                    They've made it again,
Which means the globe's still working, the
        Creation's
Still waking refreshed, our summer's
Still all to come—
                    And here they are, here they are
                        again
Erupting across yard-stones
Shrapnel-scatter terror. Frog-gapers,
Speedway goggles, international mobsters—

A bolas of three or four wire screams
Jockeying across each other
On their switchback wheel of death.
They swat past, hard-fletched,

Veer on the hard air, toss up over the roof
And are gone again. Their mole-dark labouring,
Their lunatic limber scramming frenzy
And their whirling blades

Sparkle out into blue—
                    Not ours any more.
Rats ransacked their nests, so now they shun us.
Round luckier houses now
They crowd their evening dirt-track meetings

Racing their discords, screaming as if speed-burned,
Head-height, clipping the doorway
With their leaden velocity and their butterfly
        lightness,
Their too-much power, their arrow-thwack into the
        eaves.

Every year a first-fling nearly-flying
Misfit flopped in our yard,
Groggily somersaulting to get airborne.
He bat-crawled on his tiny useless feet, tangling his
        flails,

75

Like a broken toy, and shrieking thinly
Till I tossed him up—then suddenly he flowed away
    under
His bowed shoulders of enormous swimming power,
Slid away along levels wobbling

On the fine wire they have reduced life to,
And crashed among the raspberries.
Then followed fiery hospital hours
In a kitchen. The moustached goblin savage

Nested in a scarf. The bright blank
Blind, like an angel, to my meat-crumbs and flies.
Eyelids resting. Wasted clingers curled.
The inevitable balsa death.

               Finally burial
For the husk
Of my little Apollo—

The charred scream
Folded in its huge power.

                                        Ted Hughes

Winter Birds

Most mornings now they're there,
Humped on the chestnut fence
Awaiting the regular hour
That brings me out of the shower,
Warm, pulling on my pants,
Enjoying a last yawn.
They might have been there since dawn,

And have been for all I know.
So I crumble up their bread
As a famished one or two
Hop down on to the snow—
Thrushes, all bold eye
And cream and coffee feather.
How they confront the weather!

It is habit, I suppose,
That brings these birds to wait,
And the natures that they all
So variously inherit
Show up as they strut and eat—
These starlings now, they call
Their friends to share the meal.

And when all seems to have gone
An elegant wagtail comes,
Turning his slender neck
And precise, selective beak
To feed on specks so small
They seem not there at all.
He eats the crumbs of crumbs.

But the harsh, predatory,
Scavenging, black-headed gulls
Uncertainly wheel and call,
Or balefully sit in the field.
Though fiercely hunger pulls
They will not come for the bread
And fly at the lift of my head.

But it is the gulls I hear
As I take the car down the road,
Their voices cold as winter,
Their wings grey as a cloud.
They've had nothing from my hands,
And I wish before dark fall
Some comfort for us all.

Leslie Norris

Tomcat

While others were curled on their evening rugs
or purring on laps to a loving stroke,
this one was loosening dustbin-lids
to get at the fish-heads. With a rattle and crash
he'd dive in to select the garbage.

77

We say we like cats for their coldness,
seeing in their chill the slow dignity
we wish we possessed—no messy affection there,
nothing of slop to bring a rift
between Tom and his lessons in reality.

We had a blackbird family in a laurel hedge.
He waited on the wall for treacherous dusk,
squeezed through the branches and murdered the mother
and chicks. We saw the red feathered remnant, scattered
in a raging minute from life to gobbling death.

Those like him that lope in predatory dark
are men's men, criminals looting on the run.
If they see a hot cat on a roof, sex is the second choice
to a guzzling kill. His ancestors lived on farms,
the equal of anything vicious on four fast legs.

His history was probably short, a panther thrown out
from a series of heaving litters
stinking in a barnyard of cat orgy—
his mother and brothers drowned in a shuttered barrel.
Flung in a ditch, he began with grass-high vision.

He stared at the battlefield, grew bigger on mouse and sparrow,
checked the competition and liked what he saw.
No pamper of milk came to soften him,
human hands were to spit and bite at.
When he arrived in our garden, his pessimism was quite complete.

No one ever called him pussy, except old ladies
fuddled in sentiment. A black scavenging scrag,
for a month he shocked birds from the lanes,
rummaging wherever a stench was pleasing
and lodging on a sack in a shed.

There they found him, asleep, and clubbed him to a pulp.
He wouldn't taste full cream now, or caviare from tins.
Lean aloof prowler, he deserved no catafalque.
But after they threw him in a pit, I put him on a spade
and buried him under a scarecrow hanging in the wind.

John Tripp

Badger

Harmless they call him, a lovable nocturnal thing,
a family man spending daylight in his deep sett.
He has an old reputation for remaining aloof.
I thought he stuffed himself on insects and roots,
a fallen egg, a few mice, nothing his own size.
But from a cable-drum he came sniffing for our buck
after dark, baiting him and scratching at the mesh,
then deadly serious one night with his big jaws
and his bone-crushing molars rampant.
He wanted much more than a boring vegetable dish.

Grizzled snouter with the claws and thick white stripe,
he scooped a hole under the boxwood hutch,
splintered the floor with his ramming head
and then clambered up and through it.
Our poor young rabbit must have died of fright
but not before the badger minced him
into string and red slippery pulp.
That lovable thing left a smear of blood and droppings
on a mile-long strip of hutch and run
before a smallholder blew his head off.

John Tripp

Foxes' Moon

Night over England's interrupted pastoral,
    And moonlight on the frigid lattices
Of pylons. The shapes of dusk
    Take on an edge, refined
By a drying wind and foxes bring
    Flint hearts and sharpened senses to
This desolation of grisaille in which the dew
    Grows clearer, colder. Foxes go
In their ravenous quiet to where
    The last farm meets the first
Row from the approaching town: they nose
    The garbage of the yards, move through
The white displacement of a daily view
    Uninterrupted. Warm sleepers turn,
Catch the thin volpine bark between
    Dream on dream, then lose it

79

To the babbling undertow they swim. These
   Are the fox hours, cleansed
Of all the meanings we can use
   And so refuse them. Foxes glow,
Ghosts unacknowledged in the moonlight
   Of the suburb, and like ghosts they flow
Back, racing the coming red, the beams
   Of early cars, a world not theirs
Gleaming from kindled windows, asphalt, wires.

Charles Tomlinson

The Stag

While the rain fell on the November woodland shoulder of Exmoor
While the traffic jam along the road honked and shouted
Because the farmers were parking wherever they could
And scrambling to the bank-top to stare through the tree-fringe
Which was leafless,
The stag ran through his private forest.

While the rain drummed on the roofs of the parked cars
And the kids inside cried and daubed their chocolate and fought
And mothers and aunts and grandmothers
Were a tangle of undoing sandwiches and screwed-round gossiping
                                    heads
Steaming up the windows,
The stag loped through his favourite valley.

While the blue horsemen down in the boggy meadow
Sodden nearly black, on sodden horses,
Spaced as at a military parade,
Moved a few paces to the right and a few to the left and felt rather
                                      foolish
Looking at the brown impassable river,
The stag came over the last hill of Exmoor.

While everybody high-kneed it to the bank-top all along the road
Where steady men in oilskins were stationed at binoculars,
And the horsemen by the river galloped anxiously this way and that
And the cry of hounds came tumbling invisibly with their echoes
                       down through the draggle of trees,
Swinging across the wall of dark woodland,
The stag dropped into a strange country.

And turned at the river
Hearing the hound-pack smash the undergrowth, hearing the bell-
note
Of the voice that carried all the others,
Then while his limbs all cried different directions to his lungs, which
only wanted to rest,
The blue horsemen on the bank opposite
Pulled aside the camouflage of their terrible planet.

And the stag doubled back weeping and looking for home up a valley
and down a valley
While the strange trees struck at him and the brambles lashed him,
And the strange earth came galloping after him carrying the
loll-tongued hounds to fling all over him
And his heart became just a club beating his ribs and his own hooves
shouted with hounds' voices,
And the crowd on the road got back into their cars
Wet-through and disappointed.

Ted Hughes

Grass

I walk on grass more often
Than most men. Something in me
Still values wealth as a wide field
With blades locked close enough
To keep soil out of mind. It is a test
Of grass when I push a foot
Hard on its green spring. The high pastures
I mean, open to the unfenced wind,
Bitten by sheep.

Go into Hereford,
My grandfather said, (his dwarf
Grass was scarce as emeralds,
The wet peat crept brown into his happiness),
In Hereford the grass is up to your waist.
We could not gather such unthinkable richness,
We stared over the scraped hill to luscious England.

Behind us the spun brook whitened
On boulders, and rolled, a slow thread
On the eyes, to bubbling pebbles.

I have been in wet grass up to the waist,
In loaded summer, on heavy summer mornings,
And when I came away my clothes, my shoes,
My hair even, were full of hard seeds
Of abundant grass. Brushes would not remove them.

Winters, I know grass is alive
In quiet ditches, in moist, secret places
Warmed by the two-hour sun. And as the year
Turns gently for more light,
Viridian grass moves out to lie in circles,
Live wreaths for the dying winter.

Soon roots of couch-grass,
Sly, white, exploratory, will lie
Bare to my spade. Smooth and pliable,
Their sleek heads harder
And more durable than granite.
It is worth fighting against grass.

Leslie Norris

Weeds

Some people are flower lovers.
I'm a weed lover.

Weeds don't need planting in well-drained soil;
They don't ask for fertilizer or bits of rag to scare away birds.
They come without invitation;
And they don't take the hint when you want them to go.
Weeds are nobody's guests:
More like squatters.

82

Coltsfoot laying claim to every new-dug clump of clay;
Pearlwort scraping up a living from a ha'porth of mortar;
Dandelions you daren't pick or you know what will happen;
Sour docks that make a first-rate poultice for nettle-stings;
And flat-foot plantain in the back street,
    gathering more dust than the dustmen.

Even the names are a folk-song:
Fat hen, rat's tail, cat's ear, old men's baccy and Stinking
    Billy
Ring a prettier chime for me than honeysuckle or jasmine,
And Sweet Cicely smells cleaner than Sweet William though
    she's barred from the garden.

And they have their uses, weeds.
Think of the old, worked-out mines—
Quarries and tunnels, earth scorched and scruffy,
    torn-up railways, splintered sleepers,
And a whole Sahara of grit and smother and cinders.

But go in summer and where is all the clutter?
For a new town has risen of a thousand towers,
Sparkling like granite, swaying like larches,
And every spiky belfry humming with a peal of bees.
Rosebay willowherb:
Only a weed!

Flowers are for wrapping in cellophane to present as a
    bouquet;
Flowers are for prize-arrangements in vases and silver
    tea-pots;
Flowers are for plaiting into funeral wreaths.
You can keep your flowers.
Give me weeds!

Norman Nicholson

Toadstools

October is springtime
For mushrooms and toadstools,
For mole-hill rings
Of Parasol, Snow Bonnet,
Ink Cap and Death Cap,
Beef-steak and burnt-out
King Alfred Cakes.
You may not care a rap
What name each takes,
But eat the wrong one
And you'll soon know you've done it.
Flitters and off-comes
Of ground-damps and dews;
Chlorophyll-lackers,
Slackers and shirkers,
Puff-lumps with no green
Blood in their veins;
Plants that toil not,
That never learn to
Earn their daily
Crumbs of sun;
White octopus-threads,
Under bark, under soil,
That suck dear death
Out of petal and frond,
With never a summering,
Never a giving
Of pollen or seed—
But a parasite-toll
On the whole green set-up.
There are more species
Of moulds and fungi
Than of all the flowering
Plants of the earth—
And the flowers, under lowering
Back-end skies,
Dying, admit:
It's one way of living.

Norman Nicholson

84

Scafell Pike

Look
Along the well
Of the street,
Between the gasworks and the neat
Sparrow-stepped gable
Of the Catholic chapel,
High
Above tilt and crook
Of the tumbledown
Roofs of the town—
Scafell Pike,
The tallest hill in England.

How small it seems,
So far away,
No more than a notch
On the plate-glass window of the sky!
Watch
A puff of kitchen smoke
Block out peak and pinnacle—
Rock-pie of volcanic lava
Half a mile thick
Scotched out
At the click of an eye.

Look again
In five hundred, a thousand or ten
Thousand years:
A ruin where
The chapel was; brown
Rubble and scrub and cinders where
The gasworks used to be;
No roofs, no town,
Maybe no men;
But yonder where a lather-rinse of cloud pours down
The spiked wall of the sky-line, see,
Scafell Pike
Still there.

Norman Nicholson

War

Perplexed by the Sunlight

The boy is perplexed by the sunlight:
after four days of sheltering
underground, outside the village,
he wanders homeward, to meet
chaos: the dead cattle, voices chattering,
the first fires being relit after the barrage.

Turning slowly above the delta,
the pilot edges over the green map
his silver triangle. Perplexed by the sunlight,
he only half-attends to the navigator,
is half-surprised to feel the cargo drop
and plane leap sunward; he cannot see the target.

Grevel Lindop

Streets

The poem was entitled 'The Streets of Hanoi',
It told of falling bombs and death and destruction
And misery and pain and wastage.
The poem was set to music, which told of death
And destruction and misery and pain and wastage.

A hall was found to play it in, a singer to sing it,
An orchestra to accompany the singer, and a printer
To print the programme . . . Whereupon it was felt
(Things being what they happened to be) that
The song had better be called 'The Streets of Saigon'.

It was well sung, well played, and well received.

Truly poetry is international, just like music,
And falling bombs and death and destruction
And misery and pain and wastage,

Truly we only need one poet in the world
Since local references can be inserted by editors,
Theatre managers or clerks in the Culture Ministries.

D.J. Enright

Communiqué to a Child

First of all you must not complain.
The bomb that blew off your left leg,
and tore away one of your eyes,
was placed by some of our volunteers
to obtain maximum psychological effect
in the struggle to achieve our demands.
It was not our intention to maim
or kill anyone, and we regret the death
of your mother. However, you must
accept that there are no innocents
in a situation such as this.
So, adjust to your present condition,
and do not condemn us. As you
limp into the future your one eye
will enable you to see things clearly,
and you will evaluate the event
with the wisdom of age. You will
begin to understand why it happened.
Only an adult can possibly know this,
and apply reason to the suffering.

Jim Burns

Pictures in the Papers

Bewildered girl, her vulnerable face
reflecting nightmare war, her little hand
in bloodstained bandage inexpertly dressed,
she limps along half leaning on a stick,
her wound ill bound in military haste,
parents already dead in battle wreck
of jungle town now named as Dong Xoai.

And sadder pictures that could make you cry:
grim soldiers shoot deserters in a ditch,
cold blooded, singly, while the others watch;
emaciated mother, staring wild
and streaming tears, enfolds her murdered child.

The poetry, he said, is in the pity.
We need another Wilfred Owen now.

Tom Earley

An Interim

I

While the war drags on, always worse,
the soul dwindles sometimes to an ant
rapid upon a cracked surface;

lightly, grimly, incessantly
it skims the unfathomed clefts where despair
seethes hot and black.

II

Children in the laundromat
waiting while their mothers fold sheets.
A five-year-old boy addresses
a four-year-old girl. 'When I say,
Do you want some gum? say *yes*.'
'Yes . . .' 'Wait!—Now:
Do you want some gum?'
'Yes!' 'Well yes means no,
so you can't have any.'
He chews. He pops a big, delicate bubble at her.

O language, virtue
of man, touchstone
worn down by what
gross friction . . .

           And,
' "It became necessary
to destroy the town to save it,"
a United States major said today.
He was talking about the decision
by allied commanders to bomb and shell the town
regardless of civilian casualties,
to rout the Vietcong.'

O language, mother of thought,
are you rejecting us as we reject you?

Language, coral island
accrued from human comprehensions,
human dreams,

you are eroded as war erodes us.

Denise Levertov

Battlefields

Tonight in the pub I talked with Ernie Jones
Who served with the Somersets in Normandy,
And we remembered how our fathers told
The sad and muddy legends of their war,
And how, as youngsters, we would grin and say:
'The old man's on his favourite topic now,
He never tires of telling us the tale.'
We are the old men now, our turn has come.
The names have changed—Tobruk and Alamein,
Arnhem, the Falaise Gap and Caen Canal
Displace the Dardanelles, Gallipoli,
Vimy Ridge, the Somme—but little else.

Our children do not want to hear about
The days when we were young and, sometimes, brave,
And who can blame them? Certainly not us.
We drank a last half pint and said goodnight.
And now, at home, the family is in bed,
The kitchen table littered with crashed planes;
A tank is tilted on its side, one track
Has been blown off; behind the butter-dish
Two Gunners kneel, whose gun has disappeared;
A Grenadier with busby and red coat
Mounts guard before a half a pound of cheese.
Some infantry with bayonets fixed begin
A slow advance towards the table edge.
Conscripted from another time and place
A wild Apache waves his tomahawk.
It's all a game. Upstairs, my youngest son
Roars like a little Stuka as he dives
Through dream, banks steep, then cuts his engine out,
Levels, re-enters the armistice of sleep.

Vernon Scannell

War Cemetery, Ranville

A still parade of stone tablets,
White as aspirin under the bland
Wash of an August sky, they stand
In exact battalions, their shoulders square.

I move slowly along the lines
Like a visiting Commander
Noting each rank, name and number
And that a few are without names.

All have been efficiently drilled,
They do not blink or shift beneath
My inspection; they do not breathe
Or sway in the hot summer air.

90

The warmth is sick with too much scent
And thick as ointment. Flowers hurt,
Their sweetness fed by dirt,
Breathing in the dark earth underneath.

Outside the cemetery walls
The children play; their shouts are thrown
High in the air, burst and come down
In shrapnel softer than summer rain.

Vernon Scannell

The Black and the White

Sinking on iron streets, the bin-lid
-shielded, battleship-grey-faced kids

Shinny up the lamp post, cannot tear
Themselves away, refuse to come in

From the dying lost day they douse
With petrol and set the town's holy

Cows on fire, as if the burning bus
                    or car
Could light up their eyes ever, much
                            less
The burning of our own kitchen houses

Coming over the TV screen had held
Any surprises, for really, we wallow
                    in this old

Time western where the 'savages' are
                        bad
And lost the war because
                the white men
Always have to be the Good Guys.

Padraic Fiacc

Enemy encounter

Dumping (left over from the autumn)
dead leaves, near a culvert
I come on
        a British Army Soldier
with a rifle and a radio
perched, hiding. He has red hair.

He is young enough to be my weenie
-bopper daughter's boy-friend.
He is like a lonely little winter robin.

We are that close to each other, I
can nearly hear his heart beating.

I say something bland to make him grin
but his glass eyes look past my side
-whiskers down
        to the Shore Road street
I am an Irish man
        and he is afraid
that I have come to kill him.

Padraic Fiacc

Waterloo

Waterloo? We went once.
There were several hours to fill
before we caught the boat.
A pyramidal, man-made hill
climbs greenly where the prince
of Orange took his final spill.

I didn't know before
that any Dutch were near the place.
I'd always thought it was
just French and Prussians face to face—
and the English of course,
that other violent race.

92

All have their cenotaphs
praising the field on which they bled,
but wheat—like the grand army
accoutred, bright and high of head—
is their true memorial,
dunged by forty thousand dead.

China Wellington boots,
Napoleons, sell briskly here.
What Waterloo was for
the diorama makes quite clear—
the royal Belgian
tourist industry, it would appear.

Raymond Garlick

Towton

They crossed the river at the cooling towers
Where slipper-shaped barges carrying coal
Are tidied against the power station wharf.
It was not the weather for going away.
Knights who played at future wars, pedalling
Tanks of armour, and soldiers with leaden mallets
To mash men's brains distinct from the screaming mind
Came over that river polluted, since, with everything
And, then, with nothing but blood. They crossed the A1's
Dual carriageways. It was bitter.
Easter was late that year. They traversed the woods
Where every Autumn in fits of generosity
The wind throws down horse chestnuts to waiting children
And every Spring leaves work their fingers
Out of the bud and into a glove of warmer air.
They had to be killed by tens of thousands to erect
A small stone cross beside a minor road
Within the museum calm of farming land,
Part of a plain where the signs of battles
Cross their swords on the map like a military wedding
And birds of carrion queued for the warriors
Doomed to death from earliest recorded times.
Couldn't Palm Sunday in 1461
Have been remembered just for its having snowed?
War like love puts under the microscope

93

Some undistinguished bush that shelters it;
On that bitter day anonymous snowflakes
Stained with blood were magnified in battle.
Perhaps in a way it was saddest
Not that son killed father and vice versa
In the melodramatic early Shakespearean style
And not that former 'friend' killed former 'friend'
But saddest that, as usual, men killed strangers,
Mercenaries, turncoats, and husbands
Of widows and fathers of orphans,
Meaningless to those who worked on them.

Stanley Cook

Space

To the Moon and Back

countdown	takeoff
moonprints	rockbox
splashdown	claptrap

William Plomer

Sputnik

Before I saw my first
Sputnik I'd seen, that morning,
Two very old men repairing
A bit of dry-stone wall
In a dalehead lane whose signpost
Said: 'Impassable for motors'.

Not stopping, levering more
Than a man's weight, one said
'Last night, did you see that sputnik?'
And went on working. My child
Stayed up as it grew dark
To see 'a shooting star'.

He shrugged the sputnik off
In boredom as it flared by
And went to bed frustrated.
It was my luck to see
'A shooting star' not long
After the sputnik passed.

I thought as I saw the meteor
Burn out in our atmosphere
Of my child's world asleep
And of those two old craftsmen.
I had no grandiose thoughts
Of ten thousand technologists,

But pondered as I saw
The regimen of air
Invaded so, and looked
At the pole star and the wall
And wished for a world so steered
Levered back repaired
For a child to wake in safe.

Patric Dickinson

Cape Kennedy

Contractors, plastic-hatted, stride about
The metal-fretted sites. Launchpads
Disintegrate. Already rocketry
Seems gone with the time-clock. Picking your way
Complex to complex here where distant surf
Pounds on a whitesand shore, you stir
Among ghosts. This sterile flat terrain
Home of the thorn, scrub, swamp,
Blossomed but yesterday
With structures, artifacts
Of a new-moon-age. Now dwindles in decay.

Grass spurts. The gantries rust.
Success, disaster sped into the past.
Papers, the quick-look data float around
Flogged along concrete in a wrecker's yard.
Debris kicked up at each foot's impetus
Jogs memory. The famous missile names
Squat Matador, Polaris, Vanguard long
Forgotten come again to mind. Spacecraft
Gemini, Mariner, Apollo
Flown with a far-from-equable wind.

Salt loads, invades the air. The white paint
Blisters in a dusty shower. Space-history
Compressed into a brief decade has left no name,
The flying minute telescoped
Into a flash of time, a trail of flame.

M.A.B. Jones

The Moon

Now from our village we regard the moon
prime satellite, that some have visited,
a place like Venice but more surely dead,
with less to offer at its broadest noon
than thirty seconds here in any June;
its sole surprise the black sky overhead;
this, after all the peering poets said,
will mean no more than buoy or bollard soon.

Now stripped of mischief if it's glimpsed through glass,
a neutral disc hereforth, although its light
lays waning magic on tree-shadowed grass,
that fabulous tub of myth and metaphor
still rules the seas with undiminished might
and daily hurls the tides against the shore.

John Hewitt

Moon Rapture

Tonight the captured moon
Pouring her liquid silver over walls
Trees, buildings, patines inside floors
With candid light. At sight of her
High-riding over houses, mountains, moors
Clouds headstrong, boisterous
I can forget
The battery of silent armament
Assembled there. I can discard
News of soft landings, spacecraft
Circling insignificant earth
Soon to set off to the nearest stars.

And though I know
That unmanned capsules now explore
The solar system, may resolve
Unfathomed mysteries, tonight
My world drenched in this alabaster light
I can remember love
Among the ancient gods, Mount Latmos, myth
Think of romance, Endymion.

M.A.B. Jones

Something is Happening

Dead or not
the star is signalling,
at Jodrell Bank
the needle is still jumping.
Here and now
it happened yesterday
and then and there
it will arrive tomorrow.

Tambourine,
bell, steeple,
stained glass window,
Torquemada
Moody and Sankey
and the rector who
was killed in
a lion's cage

Are shaken by
refracted messages.
In other time
something is happening,
the stone is dropped,
the waves are rippling
and here and now
the news is still arriving.

Sydney Carter

98

The Choice

They were landing and the great thrust
Pressed like magnetism on their bodies.
The silver ship hovered then slowly
Dropped on meadow grass.

Starglyn, the captain, stared
At the green landscape.
Between two hills a deserted city,
Crumbling and overgrown, patterned
The Scanning Screen. The dials
On the Blue Screen indicated
No human life present.

Suncon, the Celestial Geologist,
Smiled over his Captain's shoulder.

'You were right,' said Starglyn.
'They must have been a very aggressive people.
What was your main source of information?'

'The great meteorite which broke
From Earth in 2048 A.D.
We took it to Station Z
And examined it.
It told us everything.'

'What?' asked Starglyn.

'They were allowed to choose
Between good and evil
And they chose evil . . .'

'Bloody fools,' muttered Starglyn.

Robert Morgan

Verdict

What now with slow and clumsy pride we make—
Space-suit and module, lunar vehicle—
To you, our children, will most surely look
Ridiculous: no Man-made Miracle,
But lonely clutter of some yet-to-be
Museum of Moon Archaeology.

You could see us now, scattering artefacts
In the timeless craters, giving them a past:
Man's mark upon those dreary-pallored crags
In gear abandoned, flag and radar mast—
Top layer in that age-old rubbish heap
Of bones and potsherds, left for you to keep.

You'll mock on archive film the awkward gait
Of our explorers, puppet Michelin Men
Bobbing in moon-walk, slow, grotesquely white,
As though pumped up with too much oxygen,
Who with their slapstick lighten the black sky
Or stoop, papoose backs tilted painfully.

Will you, controllers of undreamed-of skill,
Sophisticated, unencumbered, free
Of our dumb evolution, hard to kill,
Watch us, the stumbling clowns, indulgently?
Pity our innocence? Or turn strange eyes,
O travellers unborn, to untamed skies?

Jennifer Dines

Narrative

A Girl's Song

Early one morning
As I went out walking
I saw the young sailor
Go fresh through the fields.
His eye was as blue as
The sky up above us
And clean was his skin
As the colour of shells.

O where are you going,
Young sailor, so early?
And may I come with you
A step as you go?
He looked with his eye
And I saw the deep sea-tombs,
He opened his mouth
And I heard the sea roar.

And limp on his head
Lay his hair green as sea-grass
And scrubbed were his bones
By the inching of sand.
The long tides enfolded
The lines of his body
And slow corals grow
At the stretch of his hand.

I look from my window
In the first light of morning
And I look from my door

At the dark of the day,
But all that I see are
The fields flat and empty
And the black road run down
To Cardigan town.

Leslie Norris

Ballad

O as I span in the sunlight
  a dark lord came to me
and took me from my homely place
  his lady for to be.

He took me from step and hearthstone,
  from bower, and blaze, and bed,
to lie in his arms in darkness
  with earth beneath my head.

He took me to his shadowed halls
  beneath the mounds of green
to sit by his side and hearken
  his people call me queen.

Indeed he is more than comely
  —his skin is white as milk,
his eyes as dark as night-green sea,
  his hands as soft as silk;

and yet my heart aches still for earth,
  the mortal world of men,
where I belonged so long ago
  with rose and cat and hen.

And I who am queen of kingdoms
  that men's eyes ne'er behold
would give my soul to be going,
  as once I did, to fold
the sheep and lambs in the gloaming,
  the cattle from the cold.

Molly Holden

102

Green Man in the Garden

Green man in the garden
  Staring from the tree,
Why do you look so long and hard
  Through the pane at me?

Your eyes are dark as holly,
  Of sycamore your horns,
Your bones are made of elder-branch,
  Your teeth are made of thorns.

Your hat is made of ivy-leaf,
  Of bark your dancing shoes,
And evergreen and green and green
  Your jacket and shirt and trews.

Leave your house and leave your land
  And throw away the key,
And never look behind, he creaked,
  And come and live with me.

I bolted up the window,
  I bolted up the door,
I drew the blind that I should find
  The green man never more.

But when I softly turned the stair
  As I went up to bed,
I saw the green man standing there.
  Sleep well, my friend, he said.

                                   Charles Causley

On All Souls' Day

Last night they lit your glass with wine
And brought for you the sweet soul-cake,
And blessed the room with candle-shine
For the grave journey you would make.

They told me not to stir between
The midnight strokes of one and two,
And I should see you come again
To view the scene that once you knew.

'Good night,' they said, and journeyed on.
I turned the key, and—turning—smiled,
And in the quiet house alone
I slept serenely as a child.

Innocent was that sleep, and free,
And when the first of morning shone
I had no need to gaze and see
If crumb, or bead of wine, had gone.

My heart was easy as this bloom
Of waters rising by the bay.
I did not watch where you might come,
For you had never been away.
For you have never been away.

Charles Causley

Infant Song

Don't you love my baby, mam,
Lying in his little pram,

Polished all with water clean,
The finest baby ever seen?

*Daughter, daughter, if I could
I'd love your baby as I should,*

*But why the suit of signal red,
The horns that grow out of his head,*

*Why does he burn with brimstone heat,
Have cloven hooves instead of feet,*

*Fishing hooks upon each hand,
The keenest tail that's in the land,*

104

Pointed ears and teeth so stark
And eyes that flicker in the dark?

Don't you love my baby, mam?

Dearest, I do not think I can.
I do not, do not think I can.

Charles Causley

Time's Lovers

Lovely ladies, all are gone;
All the village girls are gone
Though the river spindles on,
Though the fox still hears the horn:
Bygone lovers lie as one;
Fox and hare and river run.

Dry, the girls who on the hill,
Let Time's lovers drink their fill:
Hunt and dance are long-since done;
Huntsmen sleep beneath the sun:
Bygone lovers lie as one;
Fox and hare and river run.

Ladies, pull and pluck the loom;
Each is risen from the tomb;
Phoenix, not a feather burned,
Each was dead, but is returned:
Bygone lovers lie as one;
Fox and hare and river run.

Shoulders, fallen sere and frail,
Flood as high as when first hale;
Shine again as white and clear
As the spell-formed atmosphere
Where the lovers lie as one,
Fox and hare and river run.

Where the body's born anew,
Where the children carve the yew,
Carve what man or mother sang,
Candle burnt, or belfry rang:
Bygone lovers lie as one:
Fox and hare and river run.

Brian Louis Pearce

The Birds o' the Parish

Spring come early, spring come late,
When the oak put on its leaves,
The martin and the swallow
Would build beneath the eaves.
But since squire 'closed the common,
Men take the road to town
And thatch where nestlings grew and flew
The wind and rain pull down.

Spring come early or late today,
The birds o' the parish are vanisht away.

Summer come early, summer come late,
The pigeon and the rook
Would lease between the women
Behind the reaping hook.
But since squire 'closed the common
And leasin's called a crime,
Men go to prison for it
And birds are snared in lime.

Summer come early or late today,
The birds o' the parish are vanisht away.

Autumn come early, autumn come late,
The ouzel on the briar
Would sing with those who hewed a log
To feed a cottage fire.
But since squire 'closed the common
And cleared it for the plough,
The poor man must burn cattle dung—
Until he lose his cow.

Autumn come early or late today,
The birds o' the parish are vanisht away.

Winter come early, winter come late,
When icicles grew on the hedge
The sparrow never lacked a crumb
Left on a window ledge.
But since squire 'closed the common,
The poor are starving so
The sparrow on the window ledge
Must stiffen in the snow.

Winter come early or late today,
The birds o' the parish are vanisht away.

Jon Stallworthy

The Centre of Attention

As grit swirls in the wind the word spreads.
On pavement approaching the bridge a crowd
Springs up like mushrooms.
They are hushed at first, intently

Looking. At the top of the pylon
The target of their gaze leans toward them.
The sky sobs
With the sirens of disaster crews

Careening toward the crowd with nets,
Ladders, resuscitation gear, their First
Aid attendants antiseptic in white duck.
The police, strapped into their holsters,

Exert themselves in crowd-control. They can't
Control the situation.
Atop the pylon there's a man who threatens
Violence. He shouts, *I'm gonna jump—*

And from the river of upturned faces
—Construction workers pausing in their
   construction work,
Shoppers diverted from their shopping,
The idlers relishing this diversion

In the vacuity of their day—arises
A chorus of cries—*Jump!*
Jump! and *No*—
Come down! Come down! Maybe, if he can hear
   them,

They seem to be saying *Jump down!* The truth
   is,
The crowd cannot make up its mind.
This is a tough decision. The man beside me
Reaches into his lunchbox and lets him have it,

Jump! before he bites his sandwich,
While next to him a young blonde clutches
Her handbag to her breasts and moans
Don't   Don't   Don't   so very softly

You'd think she was afraid of being heard.
The will of the people is divided.
Up there he hasn't made his mind up either.
He has climbed and climbed on spikes
   imbedded in the pylon

To get where he has arrived at.
Is he sure now that this is where he was going?
He looks down one way into the river.
He looks down the other way into the people.

He seems to be looking for something
Or for somebody in particular.
Is there anyone here who is that person
Or can give him what it is that he needs?

From the back of a firetruck a ladder teeters.
Inching along, up, up up up up, a policeman
Holds on with one hand, sliding it on ahead of
   him.
In the other, outstretched, a pack of cigarettes.

Soon the man will decide between
The creature comfort of one more smoke
And surcease from being a creature.
Meanwhile the crowd calls *Jump!* and calls
   Come down!

108

Now, his cassock billowing in the bulges of
    Death's black flag,
A priest creeps up the ladder too.
What will the priest and the policeman together
Persuade the man to do?

He has turned his back to them.
He has turned away from everyone.
His solitariness is nearly complete.
He is alone with his decision.

No one on the ground or halfway into the sky
    can know
The hugeness of the emptiness that surrounds
    him.
All of his senses are orphans.
His ribs are cold andirons.

Does he regret his rejection of furtive pills,
Of closet noose or engine idling in closed
    garage?
A body will plummet through shrieking air,
The audience dumb with horror, the spattered
    street . . .

The world he has left is as small as toys at his
    feet.
Where he stands, though nearer the sun, the
    wind is chill.
He clutches his arms—a caress, or is he trying
Merely to warm himself with his arms?

The people below, their necks are beginning to
    ache.
They are getting impatient for this diversion
To come to some conclusion. The priest
Inches further narrowly up the ladder.

The centre of everybody's attention
For some reason has lit up a butt. He sits down.
He looks down on the people gathered, and
    sprinkles
Some of his ashes upon them.

Before he is halfway down
The crowd is half-dispersed.
It was his aloneness that clutched them together.
They were spellbound by his despair

And now each rung brings him nearer,
Nearer to their condition
Which is not sufficiently interesting
To detain them from business or idleness either,

Or is too close to a despair
They do not dare
Exhibit before a crowd
Or admit to themselves they share.

Now the police are taking notes
On clipboards, filling the forms.
He looks round as though searching for what he
    came down for.
Traffic flows over the bridge.

Daniel Hoffman

Envoi

Along the road to Ludlow
the limes stand bright and green,
in all the meadows round them
the lambs of spring are seen.

Spring calls me to that country,
to wander in its dust.
But chance takes others westward
while I lie here, and rust.

Molly Holden

Index

Alphabetical index of poets with titles of poems

112

113

Sources and Acknowledgements

Thanks are due to the authors (or their executors), their representatives and publishers mentioned in the following list for their kind permission to reproduce copyright material:

Fleur Adcock: 'St John's School' from *The Scenic Route* (Oxford University Press).

Patricia Beer: 'The Bible' from *Driving West* (Victor Gollancz).

John Betjeman: 'Aldershot Crematorium', 'Back from Australia', 'Delectable Duchy' and 'Executive' from *A Nip in the Air* (John Murray).

Ronald Bottrall: 'Roundabout' from *Poems 1955-1973* (Anvil Press poetry); 'Address to a Head of State'.

D. W. Broadbridge: 'Camel'.

Alan Brownjohn: 'Vital' from *A Song of Good Life* (Martin Secker and Warburg).

Dennis Brutus: 'The Sounds Begin Again' from *A Simple Lust* (Heinemann Educational Books).

Arthur Bull: 'Commotion' from *Inscriptions;* 'Finis' and 'Mayflower' from *Notions;* 'Pagans' from *Flotsam*.

Jim Burns: 'Communiqué to a Child' and 'The Goldfish Speaks from Beyond the Grave' (The Salamander Imprint).

Sydney Carter: 'My Believing Bones', 'Something is Happening' and 'Tom Cat' from *The Two-Way Clock* (Stainer and Bell).

John Cassidy: 'An Attitude of Mind' from *An Attitude of Mind* (Hutchinson Publishing Group).

Charles Causley: 'Green Man in the Garden', 'Infant Song', 'Loss of an Oil Tanker' and 'On All Souls' Day' from *Collected Poems* (Macmillan).

Eiléan Ní Chuilleanáin: 'Swineherd' from *Acts and Monuments* (Gallery Press).

Cal Clothier: 'The Harbour' (*New Poetry*, Workshop Press).

Stanley Cook: 'Towton'.

John Cotton: 'New Town Blues I, II and III' from *Kilroy was Here*; 'Old Movies' from *Old Movies* (Chatto and Windus).

Patric Dickinson: 'Hornets and Adders' from *A Wintering Tree*; 'Sputnik' from *More Than Time* (Chatto and Windus).

Jennifer Dines: 'Verdict'.

Tom Earley: 'Pictures in the Papers' from *The Sad Mountain* (Chatto and Windus); 'For What We Have Received'.

D. J. Enright: 'Streets' and 'Tourist Promotion' from *Daughters of the Earth* (Chatto and Windus).

Padraic Fiacc: 'Enemy encounter' and 'The Black and the White' (Blackstaff Press).

116

Raymond Garlick: 'Waterloo' from *A Sense of Time* (J. D. Lewis and Sons, Gomer Press).

F. Pratt Green: 'The Victim Died of Stab Wounds' from *The Old Couple* (Harry Chambers/Peterloo Poets, Liskeard).

F. Grice: 'The Text' from *The Best of Scrip*.

Georgina Hammick: 'Terminal Disease, Long Sutton' from *A Poetry Quintet* (Victor Gollancz).

Seamus Heaney: 'Navvy' from *Wintering Out* (Faber and Faber).

A. L. Hendriks: 'Neighbour, Tenth Floor' from *Madonna of the Unknown Nation* (Workshop Press).

John Hewitt: 'Middle Infant' and 'The Moon' from *Out of My Time* (Blackstaff Press).

Daniel Hoffman: 'The Centre of Attention' from *Able was I ere I saw Elba* (Hutchinson Publishing Group).

Molly Holden: 'Ballad', 'Crowle, Tibberton, etc.', 'Envoi' and 'The circle' from *The Country Over* (Chatto and Windus).

Geoffrey Holloway: 'Spring She Says' from *To Have Eyes* (Anvil Press Poetry).

Ted Hughes: 'Snow and Snow', 'Swifts' and 'The Stag' from *Season Songs* (Faber and Faber).

Nigel Jenkins: 'Microscopics (Tangier, Morocco)' from *Three Young Anglo-Welsh Poets*.

M. A. B. Jones: 'Cape Kennedy', 'Chinese Acrobats', 'Moon Rapture', 'Orkney' and 'The Reservoir' from *Chinese Acrobats and Other Poems* (Dock Leaves); 'Skyjack'.

Philip Larkin: 'Going, Going' from *High Windows* (Faber and Faber).

Denise Levertov: 'An Interim I and II' from *Relearning the Alphabet* (Jonathan Cape and New Directions Publishing Corporation).

Grevel Lindop: 'Perplexed by the Sunlight' from *Fools' Paradise* (Carcanet New Press).

Norman MacCaig: 'Cold Song' and 'Sparrow' from *Old Maps and New* (The Hogarth Press).

Alasdair Maclean: 'The Buzzard' and 'The Peregrine' from *From the Wilderness* (Victor Gollancz).

Adrian Mitchell: 'Open Day at Porton' from *Ride the Nightmare* (Jonathan Cape).

John Mole: 'Recollections of a Feudal Childhood' from *The Love Horse* (E. J. Morten).

Edwin Morgan: 'Glasgow Sonnet' from *From Glasgow to Saturn* (Carcanet New Press); 'Glasgow 5 March 1971' from *Instamatic Poems* (Ian McKelvie).

Pete Morgan: 'Oil'.

Robert Morgan: 'Owen Has Retired' from *The Pass;* 'The Choice' from *The Storm* (Christopher Davies); 'September Journey' and 'Throwing Trees'.

Tina Morris: 'Tree' (Outposts Publications).

Norman Nicholson: 'Nobbut God' and 'Scafell Pike' from *Stitch and Stone* (Ceolfrith Press); 'Comprehending It Not', 'Toadstools' and 'Weeds' from *The Shadow of Black Combe* (Mid Northumberland Arts Group).

Angus Nicolson: 'the young have left' from *A Poetry Quintet* (Victor Gollancz).

Leslie Norris: 'July the Seventh' and 'Winter Birds' from *Mountains, Polecats, Pheasants*; 'A Girl's Song', 'Grass' and 'Owls' from *Ransoms* (Chatto and Windus).

Robert Nye: 'Lord Autumn' from *Divisions on a Ground* (Carcanet New Press).

Brian Patten: 'Park Note' from *The Irrelevant Song* (Allen and Unwin).

Brian Louis Pearce: 'Time's Lovers' from *Selected Poems* (Outposts Publications) and *The Best of Scrip*.

William Plomer: 'To the Moon and Back' from *Celebrations* (Jonathan Cape and the Estate of William Plomer).

Dora Polk: 'Dai Slate'.

Vernon Scannell: 'Battlefields', 'Lives of the Poet', 'Song for a Winter Birth' and 'War Cemetery, Ranville' from *The Winter Man* (Allison and Busby); 'The Poet's Tongue' from *The Loving Game* (Robson Books).

Howard Sergeant: 'Song of the Hand'.

Anne Sexton: 'Small Wire' from *The Awful Rowing Towards God* (Chatto and Windus) by permission of the Estate of Anne Sexton.

Alan Sillitoe: 'Creation' from *Storm* © Alan Sillitoe 1974 (W. H. Allen).

Jon Stallworthy: 'the birds o' the parish' from *A Familiar Tree* (Chatto and Windus).

Edward Storey: 'Unauthorized Persons, including Poets, Strictly Prohibited' (Outposts Publications).

R. S. Thomas: 'No Answer', 'The Coming' and 'The Island' from *H'm*; 'The Empty Church' from *Frequencies* (Macmillan).

Anthony Thwaite: 'Reformation' from *Inscriptions* (Oxford University Press).

Anne Tibble: 'Outside' (Outposts Publications).

Charles Tomlinson: 'Foxes' Moon' and 'Gladstone Street' from *The Way In* (Oxford University Press).

John Tripp: 'If You Ask a Welshman to Dinner' from *The Province of Belief* (Christopher Davies); 'Badger' and 'Tomcat'.

Harri Webb: 'Never Again' and 'Varieties of Religious Experience' from *A Crown for Bronwen* (J. D. Lewis and Sons, Gomer Press and Felix de Wolfe).

Evan Gwyn Williams: 'Mendin' Boots' (J. D. Lewis and Sons, Gomer Press).

Jean Williams: 'November Resort' (J. D. Lewis and Sons, Gomer Press).

Frank Wood: 'I, Sardine' (Outposts Publications).